WELCOME

In what is regarded as one of the oldest professions on Earth there is a revolution in the world of spying, both for private individuals and for governments. Technology has taken over where the human agent once reigned supreme, and no one is now excluded from investigation and interrogation. For intelligence operatives, the use of digital and Wi-Fi services by individuals has opened a new access route to lives, events, and the conversations between people, government agencies and companies around the world. Everyone can run, no one can hide.

How did we get to this situation? Was it planned? Is it good or bad? And what part do major countries play in penetrating the secret borders of potential enemies? These are questions that people ask from news reports each day which expose the inner workings of government agencies, the hour-by-hour actions on battlefields, and the machinations of politicians and political parties at home and abroad. Images flow back and forth and nowhere, it seems, is opaque to the penetrating search for rogues, traitors, and enemy agents.

In *Spies and Spying* we examine the history of this world of agents and espionage and connect traditional lines of investigating the actions of foreign states to the turbulent world of today, where so much is open to public scrutiny. Where once governments alone had access to the inner workings of closed societies, almost anyone, anywhere can turn on their screens and watch events unfold in faraway places, providing information sometimes quicker than the facts can find their way to governments.

The dark and murky world of intelligence organisations goes back several centuries, and we turn to a distant past for the origins of how spies, spying and espionage were linked to world trade and the building of empires. Moving to the last century, the 'need-to-know' about the actions and intentions of closed societies and autocracies fuelled a surge in the means of acquiring information from forbidden places in distant locations. With technology, that became easier and modern tools of observing forbidden zones from the air and from space added a new dimension and opened new doors to photographic and electronic intelligence-gathering.

But technology is controlled by humans and political or ideological beliefs toppled loyalty in some individuals working for spy agencies, causing them to betray secrets they had sworn to preserve. Some, however, sold secrets for money or personal gain, while others, lured in by a sense of importance or excitement, courted danger to satisfy an ego. Their stories are told here in addition to those engaged on secret projects who believed that sharing information was morally justified and, particularly in the case of nuclear weapons, to create a power balance, however naive that might have been.

ABOVE: President Ronald Reagan (centre) with Vice-President George H W Bush (left) and Mikhail Gorbachev during a summit in New York in 1988. (The White House)

In Biblical days, agents were sent abroad to sound-out the strength and vulnerabilities of potential enemies and it is that way today, where Russia sent secret agents to Ukraine to live among the people and discover their support for an invasion. Only in that case the message that went back to Moscow was one shaped for the ears of Vladimir Putin in the hope that when Russian troops arrived the population would succumb to force. It was not so.

In today's febrile world the need for solid, verifiable information is strong, with intelligence agencies spending more and employing a greater number of people than ever before. It is an active world where secrets are sought, agents are needed, and counter-espionage runs at high speed. These pages contain the story of how this dark and hidden world changed the course of history and created the technology that frames the modern world of espionage.

David Baker
Author

ABOVE: With intelligence information at hand, a National Security Council meeting presided over by President Reagan. (NSC)

CONTENTS

32

06

14

ISBN: 978 1 80282 969 3
Editor: David Baker
Senior editor, specials: Roger Mortimer
Email: roger.mortimer@keypublishing.com
Cover Design: Steve Donovan
Design: SJmagic DESIGN SERVICES, India
Advertising Sales Manager: Sam Clark
Email: sam.clark@keypublishing.com
Tel: 01780 755131
Advertising Production: Becky Antoniades
Email: Rebecca.antoniades@keypublishing.com

SUBSCRIPTION/MAIL ORDER
Key Publishing Ltd, PO Box 300, Stamford, Lincs, PE9 1NA
Tel: 01780 480404
Subscriptions email: subs@keypublishing.com

Mail Order email: orders@keypublishing.com
Website: www.keypublishing.com/shop

PUBLISHING
Group CEO and Publisher: Adrian Cox
Published by
Key Publishing Ltd, PO Box 100, Stamford, Lincs, PE9 1XQ
Tel: 01780 755131 **Website:** www.keypublishing.com

PRINTING
Precision Colour Printing Ltd, Haldane, Halesfield 1, Telford, Shropshire. TF7 4QQ

DISTRIBUTION
Seymour Distribution Ltd, 2 Poultry Avenue, London, EC1A 9PU
Enquiries Line: 02074 294000.

ABOVE: Queen Elizabeth I (1533-1603) presided over the first intelligence service in England, using subversive activity, codes, and spies across Europe to counter the perceived threats from Catholicism. (Lunari....m.org)

LAUNCHING AN EMPIRE

On February 1, 1587, Queen Elizabeth signed the death warrant for Mary Queen of Scots. She was accused of having conspired in a plot to assassinate the English monarch to clear the way for her own place on the royal throne in London. Her chief accuser was Francis Walsingham, considered to be England's first spymaster general and creator of a nationwide security and espionage agency which would clear a path for England's ascendancy on the global stage and lay the basis for the British Empire. It is perhaps the clearest example of the power held by informers, informants and those who employ, manage, and control them.

It is all the more remarkable that Walsingham presided over a privately funded organisation which would be hired by The Queen to protect England's interests at home and abroad in an age when this country stood alone, surrounded by political and religious enemies.

Elizabeth's father, Henry VIII had almost bankrupted the country through extravagant displays of military prowess, campaigns in France and an over-indulgence on the trappings of power. The nation was left virtually impoverished when Elizabeth came to the throne in 1558 and ruled what had been, since the sacking of the monasteries in the late 1530s, a Protestant country isolated from predominantly Roman Catholic Europe.

But Walsingham was not alone, his position as spymaster-general and protector having been ensured by William Cecil, 1st Baron Burghley, chief adviser, and secretary of state to The Queen before becoming lord high treasurer. Cecil shared with Walsingham a passionate devotion to Protestant England and the monarchy, seeking ways to trap enemies of the nation-state, defeat usurpers, and quash rebellions seeking either to put Mary Queen of Scots on the throne of England or to encourage invasion from continental powers at the behest of the Pope. With empty coffers, the nation could not afford the extravagance of a national force binding the interests of the state to the safety of the monarch and her subjects.

Two solutions were sought and acquired. The first was to reduce the risk of costly conflict by conducting covert intelligence-gathering activities to unseat rogue groups working for despots and enemy states intent on the destruction of England. The second was to encourage adventurers, privateers, and pirates to scour the seas for ships operated by enemies of England, sink them or secure bounty and loot for The Queen's war chest, which would be used to begin building a blue-water navy extending to scavenging operations across the oceans. Henry VIII had visions of such a maritime fleet of naval vessels for patrolling sea lanes and discouraging intruders but only in the Elizabethan age did that aspiration reach fruition, beginning the development of what would mature into the world's largest and strongest naval power.

Incentive for acquiring interests abroad and using trade agreements to finance a lucrative commercial operation had begun during the reign of Henry VIII when Hugh Willoughby sought a northerly route to China at the behest of the 'Company of Merchant Adventurers to New Lands'. With the intention of sailing a ship across the waters north of Russia and Siberia, Willoughby departed from London on May 10, 1553, crossing the Barents Sea and on to the islands of Novaya Zemlya before turning back for Norway. Trapped by ice, they hunkered down in their ship and were not heard of again until a Russian fishing vessel found their frozen bodies still inside the ship.

In 1555, during the reign of Mary I of England (Queen from 1553 to 1558 bridging the reigns of Henry VIII and Elizabeth I) the Company of Merchant Adventurers was re-chartered as the Muscovy Company, Willoughby's successors building a lucrative trade between Russia and England. With regular ship supplies bringing goods up the Thames as far as the Tower of London, Muscovy Street close to Trinity Square became the debarking point for sacks and bundles from Russia. It also saw the use of this company to send agents and spies to deliver messages from The Queen seeking allies and alliances. Thus began the first use in England of Walsingham's spies for developing political links connecting these two countries, with an increasingly strong bond which would remain solid until the Russian Revolution of 1917.

The Muscovy Company continued to prosper and to act as a route for shared intelligence over Russia's enemies including Sweden and Poland, the Russian headquarters known as the Old English Yard being the base of operations not far from the Kremlin in Moscow. Encouraged by student friends he met during his leave of

ABOVE: Elizabeth's spymaster, Sir Francis Walsingham, principal secretary to The Queen, brought together a wide range of skills and capabilities, including a network of secret agents to protect the monarch and to safeguard England from subversion and invasion. (John De Critz the Elder)

absence while pro-Catholic Mary I was on the throne, Walsingham assembled a pan-European group of pro-Protestant supporters in positions where they could provide him with timely updates on Catholic plans and political plots. In this way Walsingham gathered together a network of fellow travellers on the European landscape, ready to inform England of both political and military threats.

In a relatively brief period after taking over the throne of England, Elizabeth saw the opportunity for self-funded opportunists to exploit the interests of the nation for personal gain, thus saving the treasury the expense of financing exploration and at the same time planting informants across continents. In 1560 The Queen granted letters of marque to any seaman willing to raid ships of a belligerent or enemy state to plunder it of wealth and secure connections with settlement in North America, with agents of France and Spain and with other European traders establishing slave markets in foreign countries. The Vikings had introduced slavery to Muslim traders in the Middle East and now the English Crown was exploiting greed for doing the bidding of the nation using similar methods.

Among these privateers were names now famous for their audacious exploits, plying the high seas looking for foreign vessels from countries in conflict with England and securing loot for its coffers, with a substantial percentage going to the captain and his crew.

The first Englishman to circumnavigate the globe, Francis Drake is one of the more famous and well-remembered of the 'Sea Dogs', as the group came to be known, others including John Hawkins, Walter Raleigh, Richard Grenville, John Davis, and Martin Frobisher.

ABOVE: Spies and contrived letters implicated Mary Queen of Scots in a plot to overthrow Elizabeth I and she was beheaded at Fotheringhay on February 8, 1597, as depicted in this contemporary drawing by Robert Beale, who was there. (Robert Beale)

BELOW: Remains of Scandbury Manor in Kent, England, the home of Francis Walsingham (1532-1590) when he was a boy. (Ethan Doyle White)

Command of the high seas and the network of informants assembled by Francis Walsingham founded the growth of England as a proto-imperial power and while the Sea Dogs built both private and national wealth on the losses to the country's enemies, a far less obvious advantage accrued from the spy network that kept the opportunities flowing. From the Muscovy Company would be followed the East India Company in 1600, the Royal African Company in 1660 and the Hudson's Bay Company in 1670. All of these would establish colonial control on several continents and provide a network of informants and spies to keep local populations under control and England informed of subversive activity.

It did not last, with trade and settlements privately owned and operated, the flow of inward goods subsidised military defence forces in which the Royal Navy played by far the major role, leaving the army to set up expeditionary forces which prevailed largely in that role until shortly after the First World War broke out in August 1914. Walsingham died a poor man, having spent a small fortune on establishing England's first spy network and setting in train the many connections which in a later century would underpin considerable advantage to the British government. To this very day in the 21st century, many foreign countries consult with British diplomats over these historical associations which connect trade bodies to established rulers in many countries, all due to the pioneering network of contacts and informants set up by Francis Walsingham.

But there was one other, unavoidable contributor to the encroaching age of a pre-enlightenment era in which interest grew in mathematics, science, astronomy, and astrology. That man was John Dee, born on

July 13, 1527, in a modest house in Tower Ward in the City of London to Joanna Dee, wife of Rowland Dee who was a haberdasher and courtier to Henry VIII. Then in his 18th year as King of England, Henry was about to embark on a wave of change which would sweep across England and pitch it full tilt into enemies at home and abroad. In the year John was born, The King sought annulment from his first wife, Catherine, this starting a fast road to separation from the Roman Catholic Church that had for so long been the religion of England.

And so began the Reformation, when Martin Luther had thrown down a challenge to the Roman Catholic Church and introduced a new way of looking at religion.

ABOVE: William Cecil, First Baron Burghley (1520-1598) chief adviser and twice secretary of state to The Queen, presided over a foreign policy which launched the future British Empire, peppered with spies and secret agents.

(National Portrait Gallery)

It was not a propitious time to be born but John sought knowledge in a profoundly significant way by urging Queen Mary I to fund a national library in London, a depository for books, manuscripts and all the learned texts from across the educated world. His father's connections to the Royal Court brought him into contact with William Cecil and when Mary refused his appeal, Dee turned to the new-age reformers who questioned established religion and sought guidance though secular studies.

NEVER ALONE

This was a time when Nicolaus Copernicus had set bright minds alight with questions about the universe and he would soon be followed with the works of Galileo and Johannes Kepler, who explained for the first time how the planets stay in their orbits and why the Earth goes round the Sun. Dee enveloped himself with new thoughts and metaphysical postulates, telling Cecil and Walsingham that he could foretell things that were yet to happen and that he could consult with the spirits of the dead to learn the secrets of the living. That attracted Walsingham's attention and reinforced the notion that science and this new-age of learning and knowledge, aside from celestially ordained precepts, could unlock possibilities which would assist in gathering information.

In all of this, Dee, Cecil, Walsingham, and a veritable host of supporters inside and outside the Crown Court were far ahead of their time, although Dee's preoccupation with the occult and magical practices prejudices many as to his true value. Nevertheless, the society from which he sought support was a product of its age and not necessarily a consequence of

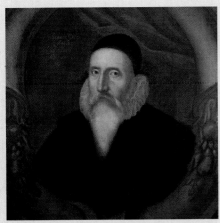

ABOVE: John Dee (1527-1608/09), astrologer, astronomer, mathematician, alchemist, and writer of codes, provided useful details for Walsingham and Burghley to establish connections between intelligence-gathering and maritime expansion. (Ashmolean Museum)

Dee's practices. At best, he is a complex figure for whom the judgements of today's society perhaps fail to take account of his questing mind in a time of uncertainty and suspicion, the very ethos of which had fuelled the equally complex world of Cecil, Walsingham, and the court of Elizabeth in establishing the framework of a national intelligence-gathering organisation.

Today, it is easy to ridicule Dee and consign his pseudoscience to the dustbin of psychedelic ramblings in a bygone age of ignorance. To do so would be to ignore the studies into remote-viewing conducted by the CIA during the 1960s and 1970s. Without scientific basis and with no verified controls to justify the belief that people could be taught to visualise the interior of rooms in buildings half a world away, one of the most advanced intelligence-gathering organisations of the modern world fell for

the arguments of misplaced advisers. In that context, we are not so far along the road of enlightenment as we like to think.

Dee was useful, and his works are worthy of study, not for their inherent truths but for the fact that he was unconstrained by conventional ways of thinking and invented new ways of addressing a challenge. And that was the basis for original ideas aroused by his insatiable desire for knowledge in an age dominated by religiosity, society's unverified acceptance of religious belief made law by the Crown. Breaking free from constrained ideas, Dee supported the use of complex mathematical formulae to create sophisticated codes and cyphers that underpinned the secret communications flowing between informants and the informed.

Walsingham and his close associates had a voracious appetite for codes and cyphers, the chief cryptographer being Thomas Phelippes who, as a multilingual graduate of Trinity College, Cambridge, had a talent for encryption. It was he who provided Walsingham with the evidence showing that Mary Queen of Scots had conspired with Anthony Babington in the plot that eventually brought her to the scaffold and had Babington hung, drawn, and quartered. Phelippes worked with master-forger Arthur Gregory who had an aptitude for breaking seals to discover written content and then resealing the document or folder with no apparent evidence that it had ever been tampered with.

Walsingham died in 1590, but his success had already encouraged Roman Catholics to form their own group of intelligence operatives, perhaps most notable being the Welshman Hugh Owen who represented the interests of Catholic exiles in an age

when the country was ruled by new-age Protestants. The legacy of Walsingham is best reflected in the wide range of informants recruited across Europe and the Mediterranean world, including the Ottoman Empire and the Middle East. This was expanded and developed over the next century from which arose a network of spies operated by Oliver Cromwell and his spymaster, John Thurloe, operating on behalf of the Parliamentary cause.

By the end of the 18th century, Britain had a large network of agents and operatives scouring the countries of Europe and Asia for detailed information on potential subversives and with France the major enemy there was considerable effort expended on harvesting military intelligence. From this came plans for the defence of coastal regions and a profound awareness that countries close to the British Isles were a potential threat. As noted previously, solid trade with Russia had been achieved through the Muscovy Company, but there were commercial interests for England in comprehensively understanding who had real power and who made the important decisions.

Key to this was Charles Whitworth, an experienced diplomat who became Ambassador to Russia in 1704 and set about consolidating the tobacco monopoly granted in 1698 whereby England would import the plant from the Americas and trade it on to Russia. But there were delicate balances in play. Russia's envoy Andrey Matveyev was dispatched to London to seek support from the English for its war with Sweden in cooperation with Denmark and Norway. London used its deep knowledge about the inner workings of Russia's autocracy to avoid involvement without offending the Court in St Petersburg.

ABOVE: Outside the town of Stamford in Lincolnshire, England, and home to Lord Burghley, Burghley House frequently hosted The Queen's advisers, secretaries of state and privateers in the expansion of British interests underpinned with espionage. (Anthony Masi)

ABOVE: The first major expedition to secure trade with Russia occurred with the formation of the Muscovy Company in 1555 out of the preceding Company of Merchant Adventurers set up by Sir Hugh Willoughby. Information obtained by spies was exchanged between the two countries until the 1917 Bolshevik revolution. (Anthony Jenkinson and Gerard de Jode)

information about Russia which would frame British policy toward that country for the next hundred years. The strong relationship with Russia would empower the logic of trying to unhinge the, albeit tenuous, grip which the Bolsheviks had on that county after the revolution of 1917. It was because of these strong Anglo-Russian ties that Winston Churchill mobilised support for the White Russians opposing Lenin, sending British troops to fight the Bolsheviks after World War One.

GUARDING THE EMPIRE

The 19th century saw unprecedented growth for Britain and her expanding Empire, but economic threats began to emerge from the United States and Germany, both of which sought to displace the United Kingdom from her lofty position on the world stage. In a century of social change, a spate of pan-European revolutions in 1848 set continental countries alight with reformist zeal that threatened the establishment. Their legacy was in the multitude of revolutionary, underground organisations working to overthrow the status quo. Challenged by zealous bands of bomb-throwing anarchists mixed in with more benign groups seeking equitability of place and rights for less privileged citizens, the security of nation-state was precarious and unpredictable.

Pivotal to the defence and security of the United Kingdom, the Admiralty and the War Office met in 1909 to agree upon establishment of a Secret Service Bureau, which came into existence on October 1. Not entirely prompted by the crossing of the English Channel for the first time by Louis Bleriot in his fragile little monoplane on July 25 that year, the vulnerability of the nation was now threatened by air, potentially at least. Those with foresight, especially the navy, recognised the advantage reconnaissance aeroplanes would have for

At the behest of Queen Anne, Whitworth operated as a secret agent for England, infiltrating all levels of Russian society to unravel its strategic potential and military capabilities. With deep knowledge of adjacent countries, Whitworth appealed to the Russian aristocracy and purported to help them better understand the world beyond the nation's border. But his real purpose was in the reverse direction and Whitworth used complex codes to send messages to London, in which were enshrined detailed accounts of the government structure and the people in Russia who controlled trade, managed production, delivering judgements on their affiliations and loyalties.

In this were sown the seeds of later diplomatic missions with a dual function enshrined within a Machiavellian purpose, his treatise on the country, its levels of rule, management and resources underpinning an increasingly comprehensive dossier of

ABOVE: Russia's Ivan the Terrible (Ivan IV) examines goods traded with the outside world as England services a regular route between the two countries, the first of an increasing number of such organisations protected by spies and secret agents. (Alexander Litvochenko)

surface fleets of any country assaulting the lengthy coastline of the British Isles. Moreover, Count Ferdinand von Zeppelin was building giant dirigibles, airships which were openly projected as the transport of the future, carrying people, freight – and bombs?

Very little progress with airships had been made by 1909 but a more prescient need arose from the wave of bomb-throwing radicals and anarchists out of disruptive groups in the Balkans and Russia, challenging the established regimes of autocracy and monarchies. There was also little awareness of the number of people arriving across the English Channel from French ports into English berths and that worried the British government, which was concerned about importing political agitators, terror-groups, and subversive and undesirable troublemakers from the European continent.

Having united into a single federated organ from several independent political states after the Franco-Prussian War of 1870, Germany had grand designs, and the British government was concerned about how those might challenge British supremacy in trade and maritime rights. To realise its imperial ambitions, Germany was funding its own equivalent to the British Dreadnought battleship, a class of warship new to the high seas and one which incorporated design and engineering features rendering all previous battleships obsolete. When launched in 1906, HMS *Dreadnought*, the first of that class, was immediately recognised as a game-changer in naval warfare, a design which was copied in a race for supremacy in the maritime environment.

For almost the entire 19th century, Britain had been the most powerful nation on Earth, but that had begun to wane and by 1909 Germany was the supreme economic power in Europe, seeking overseas territories and openly challenging the British Empire in

ABOVE: Founded in 1600 after the defeat of the Spanish Armada and the capture of its ships, the East India Company expanded England's interests through a trading arrangement policed by spies and controlled by hired brigades of British Army soldiers. (Thomas Malton the Younger)

word if not quite yet in deed. Concern about the diminishing gap between Britain and its challengers fostered a wealth of literature raising fears about German 'treachery', foreign spies, and threats of invasion, not least within William Le Queux's bestselling books *The Invasion of 1910* (written in 1906) and *Spies of the Kaiser*.

Public disquiet aroused popular concerns and stimulated political debate with outlandish convictions put about by General John Spencer Ewart, then director of military operations at the War Office, together with staffers Colonel James Edmonds and Colonel George Macdonough who plied the message that the general staff in Berlin were plotting attacks on England. After holding office for a mere 11 months,

in March 1909, Prime Minister Herbert Asquith set up a special sub-committee of the Committee of Imperial Defence to look into the purported threat. Led by Richard Haldane, Secretary of State for War, it was to examine the question of 'foreign espionage in the United Kingdom'.

Responding to outspoken concern by the general public, Asquith was, nevertheless, aware of the political challenges to his government. Pressed by fellow-Liberals Lloyd George and Winston Churchill to impose unprecedented levels of taxation on the rich and wealthy, Asquith also faced powerful opposition from the Conservatives. The display of concern for British security was a counter to accusations of inaction from the opposition party and the sub-committee included General Ewart and Admiral Alexander Bethell, director of naval intelligence, as well as Reginald McKenna, the First Lord of the Admiralty, and the Home Secretary, Herbert Gladstone.

THE NEW FACE OF ESPIONAGE

At the time there was no formal government body charged with monitoring foreign threats or acquiring detailed information on their technical and military capabilities. Since 1903, William Melville had applied his experience with Special Branch, Scotland Yard, to examine possible German threats for the Directorate of Military Operations, sending Henry D Long to Germany undercover where he reported to London on naval developments there. In 1905, Ewart's predecessor, James Grierson made a tour of the frontier between France and Belgium and since 1908 his successor, Henry Wilson, had taken a group of friends on a cycling 'holiday' along the border with Germany during which

ABOVE: James Lancaster, the first commander of the East India Company, ran an expanding empire of labour in India and the return of goods to England. (Unknown/Wikicommons)

ABOVE: In March 1909, Richard Haldane (1856-1928) set up a committee to examine the threat to Britain from German expansion in trade, weapons, and a burgeoning empire, the origin of the modern Secret Intelligence Service. (National Portrait Gallery)

they assessed potential areas where a German invasion of France might occur, noting new German rail construction close to the border.

Of equal concern to the navy was the building of the Kiel Canal allowing German ships to move from the Baltic to the North Sea without having to sail around Denmark. With the widening of that access in 1908, Germany could move its High Seas Fleet, which had been formed in February 1907 under Admiral von Tirpitz, to quickly threaten the British. In response to potential German threats, in 1904 the British Grand Fleet had been based at Scapa Flow in the Orkney Islands but, with the widening of the Kiel Canal. German Dreadnought-type battleships would be stationed at Wilhelmshaven, a bay on the eastern side of the North Sea and facing the United Kingdom.

In its peregrinations, the subcommittee spawned a further subcommittee under Sir Charles Hardinge, to look into the possibility of forming a special secret service bureau. On April 28, 1909, it presented a single hand-written report, without further copies for maximum security, endorsing the idea and recommending that such a bureau should embrace the Home Office, the War Office, and the Admiralty. It proposed that a single 'agent' be deployed to Brussels from where information obtained by spies across Europe could be collated and sent to London. It suggested that private detectives could be 'employed' to gather intelligence from other countries.

The final meeting of the main subcommittee was held on July 12 at which the recommendation was accepted but with a focus on obtaining intelligence about foreign powers rather than addressing the threat to British security, concern for which had prompted the work. Twelve days later the Committee of Imperial Defence agreed that a secret service bureau should be set up and a further meeting was held on August 26 to work out the details. A former chief police inspector, Edward Drew would work from offices at 64 Victoria St in Westminster and Henry Long would be the Brussels man.

As candidate to lead the organisation, the army nominated the highly proficient linguist Captain Vernon Kell while the Admiralty proposed Commander Mansfield Smith-Cumming. Both men went to work in the same office on October 4, 1909, with the dual role of protecting the United Kingdom and its citizens and securing information on foreign agents, saboteurs, spies, and other scoundrels undermining the national interest. At first, they divided the work between them, but each operated under the committee's conclusion that 'an extensive system of German espionage exists in this country and that we have no organisation for keeping in touch with that espionage and for accurately determining its extent or objectives'.

The two men were agreed that Kell should control the security of the country while Smith-Cumming sought information about the activities of foreign powers, insofar as it encroached on British interests, either militarily or politically. By the end of the year, Smith-Cumming, now abbreviating his surname to Cumming, had a separate office in a flat in Ashley Gardens, Vauxhall Bridge Rd, London. He had differences with Kell and when the latter suggested on March 17, 1910, that the two share the new flat together, the proposal was rejected. Cumming also protested the bias toward funding Kell's work, due perhaps to his relationship with the War Office.

Two months later, seeking an amicable solution to what was becoming a prickly relationship, during a meeting at the Admiralty on May 9, 1910, it was agreed that the two functions of the Secret Service Bureau should be separated. Kell would limit its activities to the British Isles while Cumming would look after foreign activities. Only three days previously, King Edward VII had died, and George V had succeeded him to the throne of an empire already challenged politically and militarily by continental powers. And economically too, by the unprecedented growth of the USA, now numbering 46 states, to which New Mexico and Arizona would be added in 1912.

Known provisionally as the Counter-Espionage Bureau, inside the War Office, Kell's branch was known as MO5(g), eventually MI5, and from the outset it worked closely with constabularies throughout the United Kingdom and with Special Branch at Scotland Yard, a continuous link that exists to this day. But it was MI6 that had the greatest challenges over the next several years as war-clouds gathered and Germany grew stronger. The annual budget that had been £2,000 for both services in 1909 reached almost £11,000 just three years later.

At the beginning of this period Winston Churchill was home secretary and became the strongest political supporter

BELOW: At the end of the 19th century, the development of the rigid airship by Count von Zeppelin and its military potential posed a threat to Britain's maritime trade and to the security of the United Kingdom, represented here by LZ 3 at Tegel, Berlin. (Max Missmann)

ABOVE: Stella Rimington, the first female director general of MI5, in that office from 1992 to 1996. (Andrew Davidson)

ABOVE: The Thames House entrance to the MI5 headquarters in London, the agency responsible for the protection of British citizens at home and abroad. (Cnbrb/Wikipedia)

of MI5, a government organisation acknowledged publicly, if only by inference. But disclosure was not possible for Cumming's department, the Secret Intelligence Service, or MI6, which would not be declared officially until 1986 when the Government Communication Headquarters (GCHQ) was also acknowledged. But before World War One broke out on August 4, 1914, Cumming was already facing the biggest challenge

of his tenure as the SIS came under increasing pressure from the War Office, which wanted to gain control of it, which was precisely what it had been set up by its founders to avoid.

Many believed that over the preceding centuries Britain had built on the pioneering work of Francis Walsingham, creating by the 20th century a sophisticated national intelligence service to hunt down agents and spies and conduct its own espionage and information-gathering. Myths such as this were constructs of leading novelists and authors of blood-curdling fiction, Rudyard Kipling being a particularly outspoken proponent of this fiction by conjuring up

a multi-headed organisation with tentacles around the globe.

In reality, after Walsingham, almost nothing had been done to maintain the extraordinary skills and honed practices of the quiet, Tudor spymaster who connived, lied, and tortured suspects in the basement of his own house into revealing secrets, sometimes untruths declared as fact to effect release by death from an agonisingly cruel interrogation. What had been left undone over the 300 years between these two periods was now quickly, and quietly, put together for a very different age and a set of completely different threats, to the British people and to the Empire.

ABOVE: Designed by Terry Farrell and built in 1994, the headquarters of MI6 in Vauxhall, London, manages information about foreign countries and people insofar as it affects the security of British interests. (Laurie Nevay)

FORGED IN THE FIRES OF WAR

In the 18th century, the intelligence interests of the British Empire were embodied in the War Office and in the colonial trade organisations that ran their own spy networks to inform owners of future opportunities and commercial competitors. Before 1909 and the establishment of MI5 and MI6, the British government had no formal intelligence agency and each department associated with trade, commerce, land warfare, or maritime security of the Empire employed a range of ad-hoc methods to obtain information, or to seek out agents conspiring against Britain.

With the largest navy in the world, Britain patrolled maritime trade routes across its Empire and sought to deter challengers to its eminent position in global trade and the movement of goods. It was feared by European continental powers yet confronted by countries where national interests ran counter to those of Britain, specifically during its long war with France which began in the late 17th century and would last until the defeat of Napoleon in 1815. Along with confronting French expansion in North America, the Caribbean, Africa, and India, the need for information gathered momentum throughout its possessions and territories. After the defeat of the French in the Seven Years War (1756-1763) the British imposed a tax to pay for its troops in North America, fomenting discontent.

In its colonies, insurrection, and subversion against the British simmered close to the surface as local agents and regional officials were watched for conspiracies against the establishment and Crown interests. Nowhere was this more evident than in colonies along the eastern seaboard of North America during the early 1770s. Discontented merchants eager to maximise their profits and expand continental influence over commercial and political competitors, challenged the rule of King George III. They increasingly used self-serving interests to rally support for separation from Parliament in London and the Crown.

The population of the 13 British colonies on the eastern seaboard totalled 2.2 million people, of whom it is estimated around 459,000 were black slaves. Almost a third lived in Virginia and Massachusetts, where the British had greatest concern over insurrection and rebellion. Put in perspective, the total population of these American colonies was equivalent to about 25% of the total number of people living in Britain at that time. Historians have debated the origin and motivating cause of the move for independence from Britain but uppermost was undoubtedly the desire to oppose taxation and maximise profits from the lucrative trade conducted with England. Also, to have greater power over the lives and freedoms of colonial citizens devoid of controls from across the ocean imposed without consultation.

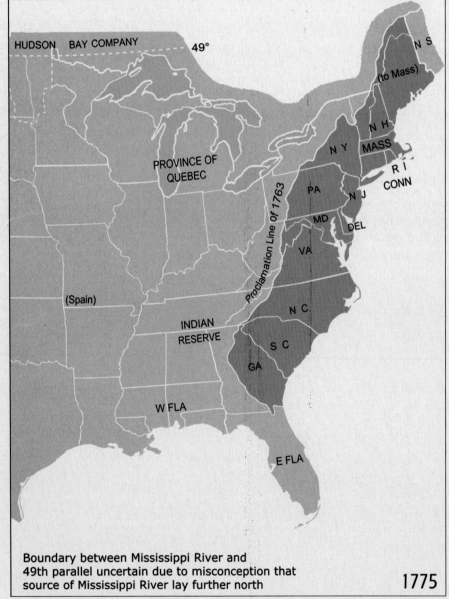

Boundary between Mississippi River and 49th parallel uncertain due to misconception that source of Mississippi River lay further north

1775

ABOVE: In the late 18th century, the 13 English colonies sought independence from the Crown in the Kingdom of Great Britain, soon to become the United Kingdom, and fought for legislative autonomy. (National Atlas of the United States)

BELOW: Philadelphia Hall where the Committee of Secret Correspondence was set up in 1775 to connect with friends in other countries supporting the American campaign for independence. (Rdsmith/Wiki commons)

Britain's concerns over the various claims on rights and privileges sought by the colonists were monitored by spies loyal to the Crown reporting on secret meetings, public speeches, and smouldering gossip on the Boston docks. As George Washington would say, "there is one evil I dread, and that is their spies." But opposition to control by the Crown was not universal although there was little opportunity to readily identify those who supported greater independence from those who did not. The trading posts, ports, harbours, and back alleys of small towns were rife with opposing loyalties as individuals and small groups met and conspired to extract greater freedoms for self-administration, even to the extent of printing leaflets for their cause.

On December 16, 1773, tea chests were dumped in the harbour at protest over additional taxes levied on imports from China by the financially troubled East India Company. That spurred a further protest in Philadelphia which sent merchant ships back to England without unloading their tea cargo. "No taxation without representation," became the common cry at the first Continental Congress held on September 5, 1774, by 12 of the 13 colonies meeting to consider their response.

In reacting to the protests, the British government had accused the colonists of treason, which brought the death penalty to individuals, disenfranchising them from rights of appeal. It used the navy to blockade the port of Boston to prevent it trading goods in or out. The First Congress barely refrained from calling for independence and petitioned The King for reason, but the Second Congress which convened on May 10, 1775, did just that, but only after fighting which had broken out on April 19

ABOVE: Being presented for ratification on July 4, 1776, the Declaration of Independence was made possible by the support from foreign countries, particularly France, for a total break with the Kingdom of Great Britain. Without that support it is not likely to have been pursued. (John Trumbull)

ABOVE: The British attack on Bunker Hill, made possible by British intelligence operatives and spies within the ranks of the revolutionaries. (Howard Pylee)

when the British tried to disarm protesters and arrest them for trial.

Thus began the War of Independence, the British declaring the American colonies to be in a 'state of rebellion'. As conflict grew and the colonies sent their men to resist the British soldiers, on July 4, 1776, the Declaration of Independence was proclaimed, authored by a group of five led by Thomas Jefferson, thereafter known as the Founding Fathers. Its most empowering tenet was forged in its second sentence: "We hold these truths to be self-evident, that all men are created equal, that they are endowed by their Creator with certain unalienable Rights, that among these are Life, Liberty and the Pursuit of Happiness."

The War of Independence would rage for eight years and four months during which the secret agents of the Crown and the newly forged United States of America supplied their respective armies with information, intelligence, counter-intelligence, and disinformation in the pursuit of supremacy on and off the battlefield. On September 18, 1775, the Second Congress established the Secret Committee which presided over the clandestine procurement of arms and munitions, including gunpowder, and carried out procurement transactions. The elaborate constructs extended to running ships under flags of convenience so as not to attract the attention of the Royal Navy.

Established by Congress on November 29, 1775, the Committee of Secret Correspondence became the first US intelligence agency and included Benjamin Franklin, Benjamin Harrison, Thomas Jefferson, and the talented crypto analyst James Lovell who would create complex codes and cyphers for the Union. It had wide and diverse roles and operated with the Continental Navy, which had been formed on October 13, initially comprised of converted merchantmen adapted for battle with ships of the British Navy. It would grow, expand, and become the United States Navy.

ABOVE: Key to following up on the secret communications between the revolutionaries and France, Benjamin Franklin arrives back in Philadelphia during 1785. (Jean Leon Gerome Ferris)

ABOVE: A formal intelligence agency was sought by Charles Pomeroy Stone when a civil war threatened in 1861, seen here in a pose with his daughter, Hattie. (Library of Congress)

The committee was highly organised, sending agents abroad, recruiting support from enemies of Britain, obtaining literature to assess foreign support in the fight for independence, and recruiting sympathisers in Scotland where the formation of the Union with England in 1707 had not gained universal support. But there were sympathisers in England too, and together with others of like mind from Wales began to form a group opposed to the imposition of additional taxation on the colonies, places where British and European people had benefitted in the trade flowing across the Atlantic Ocean. It also arranged secret meetings with European merchants and used French spies to seek support from France.

The United States would depend on trade and commerce but had few financial reserves and with the Royal Navy blockading the coast, few opportunities for moving goods by sea. It needed financial backers and support from France would be crucial to bankrolling the new country. The Committee of Secret Correspondence was frequently just that, a communication channel through which information flowed, almost always clandestinely, to and from the congressional leadership, renamed the Committee of Foreign Affairs on April 17, 1777. The necessity for a set of specific government departments to deal with such activities created the Department of Foreign Affairs on January 10, 1781, the origin of today's Department of State.

The British were less organised, and any spying was largely managed by General Sir Henry Clinton, who had arrived in Boston during May 1775 and was, by circumstances, the commander-in-chief of British forces between 1778 and 1782. The British were at a disadvantage, uncertain as to the exact whereabouts of rebel groups and unable to confront a traditional field army in the way they had been trained to

fight, and in which they had achieved results against the French in the Seven Years War. It was, therefore, essential for the British to devise a very different form of warfare, but intelligence about the enemy was crucial to success and in this Clinton had success.

The Americans were adept at infiltrating British enclaves and extracting information, establishing a counter-intelligence plan which heard several hundred cases of British sympathisers, spies and colonials subversively working for the Crown. With powers of deportation or execution, the Committee for Detecting and Defeating Conspiracies proved amazingly effective and its chief inquisitor, John Jay, would become the first chief justice of the United States.

Masters of disguise, women passed themselves off as men to infiltrate British army units, American spies hired willing supporters in England, to inform the Congress of parliamentary and military plans for the attempted suppression of the rebellion, and a wide range of diversionary tactics to confuse and distract the enemy

were developed to high level. For much of the war, the espionage and counter-espionage activities of both sides raised the sophistication in covert practices and brought new methods and processes to the arts of coded messaging and new types of cypher. Distraction was becoming as important a science as intelligence-gathering.

George Washington encouraged the use of misinformation, the deliberate publication for 'official' use of incorrect plans leaked to the British by double agents, and disinformation, false trails left in documents on the bodies of dead soldiers to divert attention from actual strategies. In several cases, by such means did the revolutionaries gain success where they were numerically or geographically disadvantaged and, on many occasions, they were able to evade capture or take advantage of uncertainty due to deliberately placed information of advantage to Washington's men and disadvantage to the British.

As an interesting adjunct to the tale of spies and espionage, the Americans used

ABOVE: The Union Army employed the skills of Allan Pinkerton for overseeing the infiltration of Confederate sympathisers and army units, here with Abraham Lincoln and General John A McClernand. (Library of Congress)

ABOVE: Allan Pinkerton could be considered the founder of organised espionage activity during the American Civil War of 1861-1865. Here, he poses on his horse for the photographer in the second year of the conflict. (Alexander/Library of Congress)

their intelligence operations to establish a base in continental Europe to support and fund the new United States. As early as September 26, 1777, Congress commissioned Benjamin Franklin, Thomas Jefferson, and Silas Deane to establish a base in France for recruiting support for the revolution. On the first anniversary of the founding of the Committee of Secret Correspondence, Franklin arrived in France to set up a station for recruiting supporters to the cause, negotiating loans from French banks, and for gaining support from a wide range of French aristocrats and freemasons.

These included Gilbert du Motier, the Marquis de Lafayette whom the Americans came to know simply as Lafayette and who travelled to America to participate actively in what he considered a grand and noble cause. Lafayette rode and fought alongside George Washington and returned to France in 1779 to argue stridently for an invasion of England and successfully recruited 6,000 Frenchmen to sail to America and fight the British, a group which he led when arriving back in Boston in April 1780. The US intelligence services made much of this and confounded British denials by placing Lafayette prominently on the battlefield along with the French contingents.

Lafayette played a large part in overturning defeats, his sprightly manner rousing the dashed spirits of revolutionary fighters, significantly reversing British successes, and achieving a military victory at Yorktown where the enemy was effectively

overwhelmed and its leading general Charles Cornwallis, the 1st Marquiss Cornwallis, captured. And it was through these actions that the value of America's first spy and intelligence-gathering agents brought direct benefit. It also set the scene for a wide, transatlantic dialogue between the revolutionary Congress and friendly powers overseas, most notable of which was France. It was perhaps the first example of how the great affairs of nations can be turned on the effectiveness of spies and agents working abroad for the common good at home.

A VERY UNCIVIL WAR

When the struggle for independence and the war with Britain that flared between 1812 and 1815 over territories to the north was over, the work of spies and agents had largely retreated to cohorts of informants and individuals seeking favour from either side, usually working to preserve their own interests. Some had passionate commitments to partisan causes, and a few worked for the good of the newly found nation. Many merely sought the excitement of high adventure, sometimes to the loss of their own lives. The structural fabric of the complex net of intelligence services set up during the revolutionary war dissipated as the nation set about its growth and expansion.

Political difference between states fostered discontent and a determination on the part of some to threaten secession from the Union, the impending

inauguration of President Abraham Lincoln on March 4, 1861, bringing plots from southern states to assassinate him and do away with his drive to expand federalism and ban slavery. Union forces were largely away in Indian territories beyond the existing railheads and there was concern about the loyalty of units charged with keeping order in Washington DC where Lincoln was to be sworn in.

ABOVE: Lafayette Curry Baker, who, along with Pinkerton, did much work on searching for co-conspirators attempting to take the life of Abraham Lincoln at the presidential inauguration on March 4, 1861. (Author's collection)

ABOVE: Rose Greenhow played an impressive role as a spy for the Confederacy, luring many Union political supporters to her residence in Washington DC where she obtained information of use to the Jefferson Davis camp. Trapped by Pinkerton, she is seen here with her daughter in the Old Capitol Prison. (Library of Congress)

United States Secret Service'. That was a title contested by Lafayette Baker, who played a seminal role in protecting the President and would lead the search for co-conspirators to the assassination of Lincoln by John Wilkes Booth on April 15, 1865.

Seeking to overthrow the Union in its control over the 11 breakaway Confederate states, Jefferson Davis had been inaugurated as its President on February 18, 1861, an event which did little to reduce the rate of escalation toward the civil war that ensued. With tensions high, the Confederates began to recruit spies and agents for their cause, a notable supporter among whom was the vivacious socialite Rose O'Neal Greenhow, who had openly wept when Davis departed his Senate seat to lead the Confederacy on January 21. But the recruiter-in-chief was John Letcher, governor of Virginia, who formed an army and organised a spy ring in the heart of downtown Washington, DC.

Greenhow used her charms to seek information from Congressional friends loyal to President Lincoln but who were unable to reject her advances, despite the political divide. Of one assignation, Senator Henry Wilson of Massachusetts complained that "spies are put upon me, but I will try to elude them tonight and once more have a happy hour in spite of fate." Drawn in too were senators from other Union states as well as Colonel Erasmus D Keyes who complained subsequently that she had "tried to persuade me not to take part in the war." Without success there, Greenhow wrote a simple, 26-symbol cipher through which she conveyed important information, obtained from her position at the centre of Union political control, out to Confederate recipients.

Greenhow supplied considerable quantities of material including letters and

The Union Army had no formal intelligence unit and when the secession began, Charles Pomeroy Stone, a recent graduate from West Point, was given the rank of colonel with orders to probe groups forming breakaway military units. Of particular concern was the National Rifles, whose commander had already proclaimed the need for his men to "guard the frontier of Maryland and help keep the Yankees from coming down to coerce the South." Concerned that this may conceal loyalists to the Confederate states seceding from the Union, Stone hired a private detective to infiltrate the National Rifles and discover their intentions. He reported back that they planned to join with 300 other men and storm the Treasury building.

Armed with this information, Stone was able to purge the volunteer organisations and eliminate one strong threat to the inauguration which, had it succeeded in assassinating Lincoln, may have completely changed the course of the Civil War. The inauguration of the President was like no other. Sharpshooters were positioned on rooftops around the capital, the

city itself 60 miles (96km) south of the Mason-Dixon line, a symbolic division between slave-owning Maryland and free Pennsylvania. Washington DC was a hotbed of sympathisers and Stone commandeered boats to prevent them being used by Southern rebels to launch attacks on the day Lincoln became President.

In their work, Stone and others used detectives from the growing number of agencies working for private clients on domestic matters, principal among which was Allan Pinkerton, the Glaswegian founder of the famous Pinkerton National Detective Agency who had emigrated to the United States in 1842. Formed in 1850, the Pinkerton Agency provided security services for companies and wealthy individuals and conducted general investigations and detective work, but during the Civil War of 1861-65 it did much work for the Union cause.

Writing to Lincoln to offer his services, Pinkerton was employed by the army as a civilian but bore the title Major E J Allen as part of his cover during the war, in which he referred to himself as the 'Chief of the

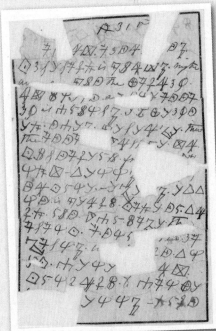

ABOVE: Greenhow used a simple but effective cypher to send information to her Confederate contacts until she was caught. (World Digital Library)

ABOVE: Spying for the Confederate cause and operating from Washington, DC, John Letcher, Governor of Virginia, became the link connecting Rose Greenhow to Confederate sympathisers. (Library of Congress)

ABOVE: Another agent working for the Union cause from a position of wealth and privilege, Elizabeth Van Lew turned her back on slave-ownership and provided valuable information for the liberation cause, paying a heavy price for her beliefs. (US Park Service)

documents as well as military information, some of which was carried by Betty Duvall posing as a travelling farm girl and driving a cart which got her through the Union lines across the Potomac. Duvall had conveyed her message in a tightly bound packet sewn in silk tucked deep inside long rolls of her hair, which she released with a tucking comb on arriving at a Virginia safe house. Some attribute the Confederate victory at the first Battle of Bull Run Creek on July 21, 1861, to information supplied by her.

Pinkerton was assigned to capture Greenhow, whose treachery to the Union was suspected from information in captured documents and her house was placed

under constant observation. One night, an unsuspecting informant arrived and observed by the agent through a high window, shared a map with Greenhow before the two moved to another room for an hour and returned arm in arm before bidding farewell to each other. The informant was followed and arrested, Greenhow's home being raided by Pinkerton a week later where documents and incriminating maps were seized.

Greenhow was imprisoned and, perhaps surprisingly, deported to the Confederacy from where she ran the Union naval blockade and travelled to France, moving on to Britain to recruit support for the rebel cause. While in London in 1864 she

published her memoirs, returning that year to North America but her ship was grounded off Wilmington, North Carolina. In the attempt to escape a Union gunboat following the grounding, she drowned. She was given a Confederate military funeral, her name immortalised today by the women's auxiliary branch of the Sons of Confederate Veterans which changed its name to the Order of the Confederate Rose.

Contrary to the notion that the Civil War was essentially begun, fought for, and decided by men, in reality women played a vital role on both sides of the conflict. One such was the wealthy heiress Elizabeth Van Lew from Richmond, Virginia, whose grandfather, Hilary Baker, was mayor of Philadelphia. Elizabeth grew up in a slave-owning family, but she supported emancipation through the Quaker school she attended and used her money to free slaves owned by rich families.

When the war began, she and her mother tended the wounded and helped Union soldiers escape through safe houses and even gave them money to bribe Confederate troops, starting a spy ring from her home. In Richmond, the heartland of Confederate support, she was ostracised and accused of spying for the Union, which she did by sending information through sympathetic 'couriers' to Washington's troops. Van Lew also built a network of agents and ran operations from her home in an audacious rebuttal to local sympathy for the South.

After the collapse of the Confederate cause and the surrender of General Robert E Lee's troops at Appomattox, Virginia, on April 9, 1865, Van Lew destroyed the diaries containing details of her agents and couriers so as to maintain their anonymity and save them from retribution. Appointed postmistress to Richmond by President Ulysses S Grant, the highest office open to a woman, she was vilified by Southern

ABOVE: Seen here in a depiction of his unit at Lookout Mountain, Major General Joseph Hooker argued the case for a structured intelligence service to serve the Union cause and made plans to set that up in early 1863. (Isaac Walton Tauber)

sympathisers and regarded contemptuously by the women generally as engaging in activities inappropriate to her sex when in reality she had offended the class into which she had been born. Elizabeth Van Lew died in 1900, a recluse shunned by locals.

WARS FOR ALL

At the end of the Civil War, several tens of thousands of slaves and free blacks recruited to the Union cause were among the dead, but they had played their part in the intelligence passed from Confederate lands. Black scouts were used to gather information as they moved through Confederate lines, and many escaped from plantations to fight for their own freedom. Pinkerton recruited a substantial number of blacks, and several confounded their masters by assembling details of local militia together with the location and strength of Confederate fortifications, tasks which they were not believed to be capable of carrying out due to their alleged 'mental inadequacy', judged by some to be only a little higher than the intellectual capacity of native American 'Indians'.

One such provider of 'Black Dispatches' as they came to be known, was free black Robert Smalls who, in 1861 rowed out to a Union warship preparing to attack the port of Fernandina in Florida to report that the Confederates were preparing to evacuate. Based on his information, Union forces attacked before the retreating Confederates could sabotage the port. Smalls went on to help the Union in other ways, notably by stealing a steamer and handing it over to them in 1862. He went on to become a Republican Representative for South Carolina's seventh district.

In many examples on land and around coastal regions, black informants faced danger and death to collect and deliver information vital to the Union cause, freed blacks working in docks and harbours rowing out to Union ships at dead of night

ABOVE: Seen here with fellow espionage officer John Babcock (right), Colonel George Sharpe put into practice what Hooker planned and that matured into the Bureau of Military Information (BMI). (Internet Archive Book Images)

to report on Confederate ships and their movements. In secret, a small number of slaves were taught to read and write, and these abilities were put to good use. Elizabeth Van Lew knew that there were no security issues with having black slaves around important documents in military households because they were required to remain illiterate by law, thus regarding them as no threat.

While Pinkerton and Lafayette Baker provided effective, but somewhat crude, techniques to obtain vital information, a more formal structure controlled by the Union army was needed. In January 1863, Major General Joseph Hooker instructed a regional commander, Colonel George Sharpe, to set up a formal intelligence-gathering service which would quickly become the Bureau of Military Information (BMI). Using covert and overt tactics, it employed scouts to collect information from Confederate deserters, interrogated prisoners, captured documents, intercepted telegraph messages, flag signals, and used reconnaissance balloons, see chapter 13, to spy on enemy positions.

The BMI was a tight-knit group, never more than 70 of whom the majority were scouts reporting directly back to Sharpe. The forerunners of today's 'all-source intelligence analysis', it collected, collated, analysed, and interpreted vital aspects of Confederate activity, employing a holistic approach with a broad-based mandate to use whatever tricks and subterfuge was necessary, not all of it legal. In June 1863, displaying remarkable talent, an escaped slave named Charlie Wright observed an enormous Confederate force under General Robert E Lee on its way through Culpepper, Georgia. Wright wasted little time in putting the information to good use.

With extraordinary detail and precision, he conveyed in detail the number of men, their equipment, provisions, weapons, and direction of travel. With stealth, General Hooker moved his troops north to shadow Lee's progress through the Shenandoah Valley and into Maryland and Pennsylvania. The information forestalled a threat to Washington DC and that could have averted a clash at the Battle of Gettysburg, which brought a serious defeat to the Confederate army and could have delayed the end of the war. Sharpe wanted Wright for his BMI, but the Union cavalry took him away and there his story ends.

Using a compilation of all-sources intelligence information, Sharpe's BMI prevented the Union army from effecting a preliminary withdrawal from Gettysburg which could have proven a disaster had not it been there to thoroughly rout the Confederate forces. General George G Meade had replaced Hooker but failed to appreciate the value of Sharpe's BMI and scaled back its operations. However, when Ulysses S Grant took over command of

ABOVE: A significant number of blacks worked undercover for the Union cause, represented here by Robert Smalls who provided valuable information about Confederate army movements around the Florida port of Fernandina. (Library of Congress)

all Union forces, Sharpe was promoted to brigadier general and used more effectively in decisions and plans based on the information he brought. After the war, Sharpe was asked to interrogate Confederate spies in Europe as to their possible involvement in the assassination of Lincoln. Appointed US Marshal for the southern district of New York, he died in 1900.

The BMI was the first intelligence organisation operated by the US Army, but it was disbanded at the end of the war in 1865 in the belief that it had no further role. In 1882 the Office of Naval Intelligence was formed, and the Army Military Information Division was set up three years later, in time to support the Spanish-American War (1898) and military operations in the Philippines (1899-1902). At the turn of the century, the US Army began to model itself on the structure of European armies and elevated the Military Intelligence Division to staff level for operations and logistics.

By May 1917, the US Army had set up the Military Intelligence Section which changed its name to the Military Intelligence Branch in February 1918 and to the Military Intelligence Division (MID) four months later. By the end of World War One it employed 282 officers and 1,159 civilians including a cryptology unit designated MI-8. Fifty French-speaking sergeants were recruited to a new Counter Intelligence Corps and that provided the basis for a post-war expansion which formed the training and planning facilities for many espionage and counter-intelligence operations during World War Two. It evolved over time, and during the 1970s into the Army Intelligence and Security Command (INSCOM) which became infamous for its research into parapsychology and remote-viewing.

AMERICA THE FREE

ABOVE: Held at the end of 1921, the Naval Conference in Washington, DC, set limits on the size of warships and became the first international gathering in which the United States used cryptoanalysis. (NARA)

In the immediate aftermath of World War One, commendable progress was made by the US Army in establishing a cryptoanalysis unit known as the Black Chamber. This was the first peacetime unit of its kind set up in the United States, operating as a commercial company in New York. It received the cooperation of US telephone and telegraph companies, one of which was Western Union which willingly turned over the messaging traffic between foreign embassies. In this way, the army, and the State Department, which dual-funded the Black Chamber, were able to keep track of who was dealing with whom in the international arena.

However, the Radio Act of 1927 put a stop to much of that cooperation when it introduced laws prohibiting access to confidential information. The idea of 'bugging' and obtaining information between government representatives of foreign powers bothered politicians where previously it had been accepted practice to eavesdrop on international telephone calls and telegrams. The cypher decoding specialists used these sources widely during the Washington Naval Conference held between November 1921 and February 1922, the first arms control conference seeking to agree limits on the size of warships in the Pacific Ocean and southeast Asia.

For this and other activities, the State Department was able to listen-in on private and confidential discussions between relevant embassy staff members which provided insight into the way foreign governments were developing tactics to evade arms agreements. Information which could not have been obtained any other way, and which had begun to expose double-dealing from several countries which appeared friendly, but which were secretly working to the disadvantage of the US. But for all its value, the Black Chamber was doomed to dissolution when Henry Stimson, President Hoover's secretary of state, became aware of its existence in 1929 and, horrified that one nation should spy on another, ordered it be to immediately shut down.

Throughout the 1930s tensions in the Pacific Ocean grew ever more threatening and when Japan invaded China in 1937 and set its sights on imperialist expansion to gain oil and rubber assets in southeast Asia the United States again addressed the clandestine methods it tolerated to ensure security against surprise attack. In early 1941 Major General Sherman Miles was given a job with General Marshall's general staff and became head of the Military Intelligence Division. His clear mandate was to use any asset at his disposal to obtain as much information as possible about Japan's intentions.

Miles wanted a group of Japanese-speaking cryptologists, but these were hard to find in the military, very few potential candidates being interested. The army was

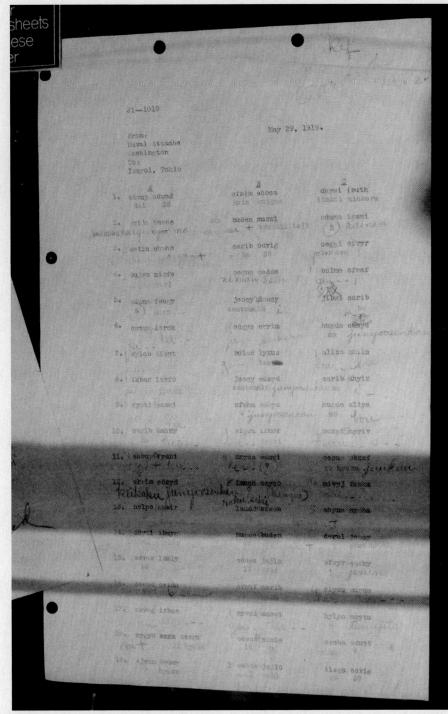

ABOVE: Established in 1919, the Black Chamber was run as a commercial company, but provided the US government with cryptoanalysis work sheets for logging communication between foreign powers. (NARA)

intelligence information about Japan's military manoeuvres and political plans for extending its influence all the way down to within striking distance of Australia. In March 1942, the MID was renamed, and reorganised, into the Military Intelligence Service (MIS), absorbing the Fourth Army Intelligence School.

Initially, the MIS had 26 people of which 16 were officers but it quickly grew to include 342 officers and 1,000 enlisted men with civilians located at Camp Savage in Minnesota. Two months after its formation, the MIS formed a specialist communications intelligence (COMINT) branch under Colonel Alfred McCormack, an attorney with special skills in this area, to obtain information from signals transmitted between the Japanese military and the government leadership in Tokyo. His remit extended into acquiring and decoding communications and signals traffic between the Tokyo government and Japan's embassies in countries still threatened with invasion. This led to a special operation involving Britain and Australia.

The Fourth Army was responsible for the defence of the western coast of the United States from where any naval or airborne attack would initially be directed. The government had few grounds to believe that Japan was preparing a direct assault on the continent but the shock over the surprise attack on Pearl Harbor raised concerns that nothing should be ruled out. The Fourth Army Intelligence School had already recruited Japanese Americans, known as Nisei, to work on staffing the school with others who could interpret the radio conversations. Usually employed on manual or menial tasks, it was a great opportunity for Nisei members of the armed services to do more productive and fulfilling work and to receive training in new skills as interpreters.

Concern at the loyalty of the Nisei permeated many branches of the armed

ABOVE: William J Donovan was appointed the first operations manager for the US Army's Coordinator of Information, set up in July 1941. (War Department)

reluctant to help him find recruits for the job, but Marshall appealed to President Roosevelt who appointed William J Donovan to set up an intelligence-gathering unit and to run operations as coordinator of information, effective July 11, 1941.

This was a separate department from the MID and brought some hostile reaction as each sought to achieve the same purpose using different methods. It did little to smooth the tracks of cooperation, much as the bristly relations between Kell (MI5) and Cumming (MI6) in Britain 30 years earlier had confused the lines of demarcation. The level of dysfunctionality between the two US government agencies played a significant

role in the varying degrees of importance attributed to information and would result in different interpretations of the same discoveries. Not least because the Office of Naval Intelligence (ONI) was also supplying the President with intelligence operations in competition with the FBI which also sought control over national security!

When Japan attacked Pearl Harbor on December 7, 1941, General Miles was replaced with General Raymond Lee, who set off on a tour of Latin America to inspect existing military installations and determine the kind of cooperation they might require. There was a clear need for a more concerted effort at obtaining timely

ABOVE: The first class at the Military Intelligence Service Language School in 1942 which trained American-Japanese to decode signals and work with cyphers to translate messages and interpret meanings. (US Army)

ABOVE: Two Military Intelligence Service officers interrogate a Japanese prisoner after the Buna campaign in 1943. (US Army)

services and anti-Japanese sentiment ran high among the civilian population, especially at the US naval bases on the west coast. Issued on February 19, 1942, Roosevelt's executive order 9066 required all US citizens with more than 1/16th Japanese blood to be removed from coastal areas. In June, the school moved to Minnesota where there was much less prejudice and eventually moved across the state from Camp Savage to Fort Snelling. By the end of the war, 6,000 students had graduated from the school.

From the outset, graduates were sent to the interrogation centres close to the front line where they questioned Japanese prisoners, but it had taken the persuasive powers of senior officers to get the interpreters out to where they could be most usefully employed. From mid-1942 to the end of the war in September 1945 the Japanese interpreters and translators had been assigned to every conflict zone.

From this grew confidence in their linguistic abilities to provide information inaccessible to most military forces. In 1943 the 442nd Infantry Regiment was formed for service in the European theatre and of 12,000 volunteers, more than 4,000 were selected for a year of training before heading overseas to become the most decorated US regiment in history.

At the end of the war, 5,000 Japanese-Americans were stationed in Japan to help administer the country and work with Japanese government officials to re-orientate the nation toward a democratic society in which they were able to play a unique part in gaining trust from the indigenous population. It did not end there, as the Japanese-Americans were key in interrogating military personnel charged with war crimes and through a cultural familiarity were able to detect bogus stories and lies used in attempts to evade

justice. Several claims have been made by senior US Army leaders to the effect that the contribution of Japanese-Americans shortened the war by two years and possibly saved up to a million lives.

MY ENEMY IS MY FRIEND

Concern about Japanese citizens and residents along the west coast of the United States reached new heights after the attack on Pearl Harbor and in more direct efforts to offset enemy initiatives through espionage and spying, on January 1, 1942, the US Army stood up the Counter Intelligence Corps (CIC). A legacy of the Corps of Intelligence Police set up by Ralph Van Deman in 1917, it re-established an important arm of the espionage business by authorising up to 4,400 personnel and 500 officers recruited from the FBI, police forces across the United States and private detectives.

The organisation was chiefly concerned with weeding out foreign agents from military or government service, and it operated largely as a military police force. The intention was to protect the armed services from infiltration by foreign agents and subversive elements attempting sabotage on bases, ports, and airfields. It also played a vital role in securing clearances for personnel working on the Manhattan project developing the world's first atomic bomb. Many scientists came from eastern Europe and Britain with uncertain loyalties and potentially compromising backgrounds.

Unlike their allied partners, even before the war the United States had been concerned about three enemies, and potential threats to US security: Japan, Germany, and Russia. While President Roosevelt leaned increasingly toward Stalin, ignoring the atrocities conducted in his name prior to World War Two, others in the political leadership and the armed services in general were highly distrustful of the Soviet Union. Security checks were made with a

ABOVE: Japanese-Americans inducted to the US Army were assigned duty in the European Theatre of Operations (ETO) and played a significant contribution to victory. (US Army)

ABOVE: The badge carried by agents of the Counter Intelligence Corps, an organisation which was also responsible for carrying out background checks on military personnel for highly classified jobs. (US Army)

view to weeding out potential communist sympathisers and exposing the practices of foreign operatives in undermining the US government at home or abroad.

A common thread throughout the 30 classified volumes recording its history was the assertion that the CIC's success in this was critical to containing communism during and after World War Two. It also had a role to play in continuing to obtain information directly from former enemy sources when the war in Europe ended on May 8, 1945. As a counter-intelligence unit it had a vested interest in securing as many former enemy officials, scientists, and engineers as possible but restrictions on bringing 'ardent Nazis' to the United States for questioning had been made by the White House. Thus, began Operation Paperclip, whereby a handful of sympathetic civil servants at the Department of State colluded with the US Army to do just that.

Initial interrogations took place in Europe but people of exceptional interest with high potential for providing detailed information on German jet aircraft, guided rockets and ballistic missiles were needed in the United States. A CIC unit was successful in identifying these people and, when a request form was sent to the Department of State seeking permission for that individual to enter the country, a paperclip was placed on the form so that the bureaucrat in Washington DC would grant permission. It was through this process that the early arrival of scientists and engineers, some potentially involved in war crimes trials, was made possible. Some of those men were vital for developing America's first battlefield ballistic missiles and other weapons.

Operating under bogus identity and disguise in liberated European countries, the CIC also ran Operation Happiness, in which former SS and SD Nazi officials

were recruited to help ferret out communist sympathisers seeking opportunities to establish controlling political parties in Western countries. With the devastation, homelessness, and migrants across the continent on the move trying to get back to their homes after displacement by the Nazis, West Germany, Italy, France, and the Low Countries were rife with extremists.

The underpinning, anti-communist sentiment in American actions sought to eliminate the possibility of extreme political causes, mobilising large groups to overthrow the restoration of democratic rule. Infiltrated by former Nazi officials working incognito, these communist cells were identified, their members recorded, and meetings penetrated by Operation Happiness in attempts to stamp out extremist groups, which the Americans saw as much on the political extreme left as they had on the extreme right, whose former personnel came to work for the Americans as informants.

In what some saw as an obsessive preoccupation with preventing the spread of communism and containing its pervasive, political message, a clandestine operation carried out by the CIC set up a rat-line, a system for spiriting out of Europe people who were either sought by the Russians, useful to American interests, or people who could be taken to countries threatened by disruptive political organisations. Informants and defectors from Soviet-controlled territories, or double-agents prepared to work in foreign countries undermining

pro-communist cells, were given travel routes, money, and places to settle in South America and other places around the world where they could provide useful services.

In Europe itself, the CIC employed former Nazi bureaucrats to operate as secret agents in Italy, Spain, and Austria, places where it was believed there could be suspicious activities, again operating against the interests of the United States. To some extent, this activity was new to Americans, awakened now from their pre-war isolationist posture, aware that it was a broken world that needed a degree of leadership which many in Washington DC believed would prevent a third global war, one which many Americans saw as a dangerous consequence of them having helped the Russians prevail in their war against Nazi Germany. The CIC was also aware that the pro-Stalin position taken by Roosevelt was now dead under his successor, Harry S Truman.

For this and other reasons associated with reconfiguring a post-war world, the CIC also worked with the Vatican in Rome, equally uncompromising of the communists, in moving former Nazi party members out to Latin America, a prime reason why so many former German military and political personnel ended up in Argentina. Some of which was supported by the Catholic Church, along with similar routes of departure through Spain. The inhumanity of former actions by people now used and manipulated by Western intelligence

ABOVE: Manzanar Relocation Center, California, where more than 120,000 Japanese-Americans were interred during World War Two. (US Army)

agencies, of which the UK and France were not immune, were balanced against the use to which they could be put in the post-war world in an effort to prevent further extreme regimes from taking hold.

But it was a delicate balance and one not without its moral consequences. Several decades after World War Two, a re-examination of those events brought certain procedures to the attention of the US Justice Department, which investigated the CIC's operations in Europe and heard testimony regarding dealings with a Croatian catholic priest who, while he was based in Rome, had worked directly for the Corps and been responsible for setting up a similar rat-line transport connection from Europe to Latin America.

In its hearings into the use of Nazi war criminals, it declassified an instruction from the Joint Chiefs of Staff to General Eisenhower dated May 10, 1945, that in holding potential war criminals "…you may make such exceptions as you deem advisable for intelligence and other military reasons". In 1950 the former SS and SD officer Klaus Barbie was secreted into exile by the CIC for fear that he would be captured and disclose all the ex-Nazi agents they had been working with positioned throughout Europe. He was eventually hunted down in Bolivia and brought to justice but not before he had been hired by the West German foreign intelligence service in 1965 with the codename 'Adler'.

The US Justice Department had a scything judgement on this story: "As the investigation of Klaus Barbie has shown, officers of the United States government were directly responsible for protecting a person wanted by the government of France on criminal charges and in arranging his escape from the law. As a direct result of

ABOVE: The US Army's Operation Paperclip saw several hundred German scientists and engineers allowed in to the United States after the war to work on classified projects, including Kurt H Debus, rocket scientist and Director of the Kennedy Space Center from 1962 to 1974. (NASA)

ABOVE: Members of the Mochida family waiting for their evacuation after the Japanese attack on Pearl Harbor drove many Japanese-Americans into the internment camps. Many others joined the US Army for work deciphering Japanese war codes. (NARA)

that action, Klaus Barbie did not stand trial in France in 1950; he spent 33 years as a free man and a fugitive from justice." Infamous for his crimes in Nazi-occupied France, where he was known as the 'Butcher of Lyon', Barbie went on trial in France and was convicted. He died in 1991 after spending four years in prison. The US government publicly apologised to France for what they had done to preserve his liberty for so long.

In further disclosure, the CIC reported having brought 765 scientists, engineers, and technicians to the United States in the 10 years following 1945, of which they believed 80% had been members of the Nazi Party. One of those was Arthur Rudolph who had been a project engineer on the V2 ballistic missile. Rudolph had presided over the fate of several thousand slave labourers assembling the rockets at the Mittelwerke facility near the Nordhausen concentration camp, where he was in charge of production. He played a major role in the development of NASA's Saturn V rocket but in the mid-1980s he agreed to relinquish his US citizenship and return to Germany.

IGNORING BARRIERS

The Japanese attack on Pearl Harbor had brought additional duties to William Donovan's Office of the Coordinator of Information (COI) which, in December 1941 had 600 people and a $10m budget. As noted earlier, there were challenges to his attempt to turn this into *the* US spy agency and the senior military leadership thought of him, a civilian, as an interloper. But President Roosevelt wanted to separate

the overt collection of information from covert operations, many of which operated at the margins of legality. So, the Foreign Information Service carrying out radio propaganda, was redirected to the Office of War Information while the 'black' arts at the COI were re-designated the Office of Strategic Services (OSS).

There was precedent for this type of organisation. On July 22, 1940, the British government had set up the Special Operations Executive (SOE) headed by Hugh Dalton, who also ran the Ministry of Economic Warfare. By this date France had surrendered to German forces and Britain was about to confront the Luftwaffe in a struggle for national survival. Winston Churchill had been Prime Minister for barely six weeks and, with British forces evacuated from the beaches of Dunkirk, had organised the disruption of German forces by conducting espionage and all manner of guerrilla warfare using specially trained operatives parachuted into enemy-occupied territory.

SOE was an amalgam of three existing British government departments: Department EH, run by the Canadian newspaper magnate Sir Campbell Stuart since March 1938 for propaganda purposes; Section D of MI6 commanded by Major Leonard Grand with a mandate to carry out all forms of sabotage in enemy territory; and MI(R) run by Major J C Holland to plan guerrilla warfare. Collectively, SOE brought together all these separate forms of creating havoc and destruction by any and all means available. The tools included explosives, devices for sending secret messages, various methods of assassination, kidnap, and

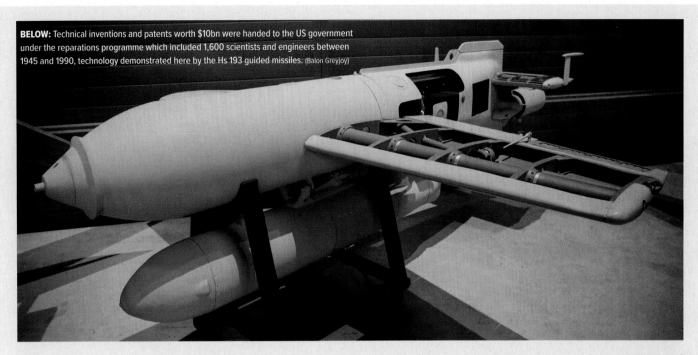

BELOW: Technical inventions and patents worth $10bn were handed to the US government under the reparations programme which included 1,600 scientists and engineers between 1945 and 1990, technology demonstrated here by the Hs 193 guided missiles. (Balon Greyjoy)

torture of enemy personnel together with the destruction of rail lines, telephone wires, and any accessible military vehicles.

A secondary function of SOE was to obtain intelligence and that extended to working in cooperation with local resistance movements to gather details and schedules of enemy activity, sent back by radio using coded messages. Important instructions to agents in occupied Europe were sent in code through open-air transmission by the British Broadcasting Corporation in London. The BBC preceded coded transmissions with the opening four notes of Beethoven's Fifth Symphony (dot, dot, dot, dash), the letter 'V' (for victory) in Morse code. SOE operated throughout the war years, a variety of different aircraft being used to put agents into occupied territory, most notable of which was the Westland Lysander, capable of short take-off and landing for operation from small fields and with a low stalling speed of 65mph (105kph).

The model SOE used was not dissimilar to covert-active methods employed by British agents operating in the United States in attempts to bankrupt pro-German businesses operating from the Caribbean before America entered the war. Prior to the attack on Pearl Harbor in December 1941, lucrative business deals were conducted by many large American companies with customers in Germany. These included major banks, IBM for its punch-card machines, known as Hollerith machines in Germany, and major car manufacturers such as the Ford Motor Company.

The German government had arranged its financial dealings through Swiss banks, as had the Soviet Union, and while many of these transactions were confidential, a good number of American businesses made considerable profit from dealing with the Nazi government and the supporting industrial infrastructure, which was spending

money on a profligate basis. This concerned the British government, where merchant ships from the United States were evading the naval blockade placed on cargo vessels sailing from North America to German ports. Cooperation even extended to German intelligence in America informing U-boat commanders which ships were carrying trade from the US, on which routes at specific locations, and which were not to be attacked.

In what many regard today as one of the most audacious acts carried out by British intelligence operatives, during the late 1930s MI6 set up an organisation in the United States with the specific aim of drawing America away from its isolationist policy while discrediting and attempting to bankrupt US companies trading with Nazi Germany. The operation began when the traditional levels of cooperation between

ABOVE: A number of Operation Paperclip engineers given work in the United States were later declared guilty of war crimes, including Arthur Rudolph who returned to Germany in 1984. (NASA)

the British security services and the FBI began to decline after the Neutrality Acts of the 1930s. These laws were brought in to ensure US isolationism and protectionism from involvement in foreign disputes and the simmering relations between distant countries.

FBI director J Edgar Hoover had maintained close relations with the British and supported continued cooperation, despite the political move to keep the US distant from foreign conflicts. There was a widespread view among the public that America should never again be drawn into a war not of its own making or not in the national interest. Central to political concern was that President Woodrow Wilson had been unable to get his proposals agreed during the negotiations formulating the 1919 Treaty of Versailles formalising the German surrender.

In the final wording of the treaty, the Americans had failed to take account of British and French interests in post-war Europe and when it was returned for ratification it was not accepted by the US Senate and under such a condition it was not legally binding. Despite the British and the French imposing its territorial boundary changes, and allied occupation of the Rhineland, Germany would use that to claim the treaty could not be legally enforced. The majority of Americans wanted no further part in European affairs, hence the isolationism which MI6 sought to break.

After the severing of relations between the FBI and MI6 when Britain declared war on Germany on September 3, 1939, Churchill became Prime Minister in May 1940 and had MI6 send the Canadian fighter pilot and businessman William Stephenson to New York in an attempt to persuade the Americans that it was within their interests to stop trading with the Nazis. With high levels of immigrants from Germany and

ABOVE: America's Office of Strategic Services (OSS) was modelled on Britain's Special Operations Executive (SOE), set up to carry out guerrilla warfare against Nazi Germany with a wide range of equipment as displayed here. (Wolcott/Wikicommons)

Italy, Britain had many enemies in the US and Hoover got the acceptance of President Roosevelt for this British operation to be given a clear path to carry out its work, which only a handful of people in America knew about.

Under the name British Security Coordination (BSC), Stephenson began work in room 3603 of the Rockefeller Center in New York, through a business registered with the authorities as the British Passport Office. British intelligence operations had been used to employing travel agencies to do their work and to serve as drop stations or coordination offices. Most notable among those being Thomas Cook, its offices in Lisbon carrying out those activities in Portugal where high level communications between senior officials from the Foreign Office in London and the German High Command in Berlin were exchanged, a channel through which contact could be maintained in the heat of war.

Clandestine channels are vital conduits in war and always exist. Even today there are continuous lines of communication between British officials in London and their opposite numbers in the Kremlin, especially important during the present conflict over territory in Ukraine, if only to avoid inadvertent misunderstanding about the use of chemical, biological or nuclear weapons. But in the United States during 1940, Stephenson and his small team, among whom was espionage agent Ian Fleming, later a novelist and author of the James Bond spy thrillers, set to work creating a clandestine operation in support of British interests and under the direct instructions of the Prime Minister.

For 18 months they sought out and exposed German spies working in America to whip up support for the Nazi cause, most infamous of whom was Gerhard Alois Westrick who had represented ITT, Ford, General Motors, Standard Oil, and the Texas Oil Company in Germany, while assuring corporate executives that after the war his country and Japan would preside over a global economy and that American participation in that would serve them well. The press contacts of Sir Campbell Smith came in particularly useful whenever it was

ABOVE: SOE dropped spies, agents, and saboteurs into Nazi-occupied Europe using the Westland Lysander, among other aircraft. (Paul Maritz)

ABOVE: The British Security Coordination (BSC) was set up with headquarters in 60 Fifth Avenue, New York, to sever links between American trading companies and Nazi Germany. (Sami99TRwikimedia)

British officials trying to buy munitions and war equipment from the Americans. By inserting themselves in the lines of communication between these groups, German agents could upset the deals, inform Berlin of negotiations, and even plot the sinking of merchant ships carrying freight to British ports. This became of concern to the Admiralty in London and to RAF Coastal Command who did not have the means at this stage of the war to conduct airborne sweeps far out in the Atlantic Ocean.

There was even a link between the Irish Republican Army and German intermediaries to sound out the possibility of German submarines refuelling on the south and west coasts of Ireland. This would have been difficult given the quantities of fuel required and the tedium of carrying out such work under hazardous conditions. There has never been a shred of evidence to prove that these refuelling activities actually took place, although there is a lot of anecdotal evidence that German submariners left their boats moored in remote bays on Moonless nights and came ashore on inflatables, relaxing for several hours in remote pubs over a pint or two of Guinness and Irish hospitality!

Increasingly, throughout 1940 and 1941, the British sought to use Stephenson's BSC for a softly-softly approach to persuasive use of black propaganda and misinformation. They wanted to transmit information between a training camp in Canada and London, and the Political Warfare Executive needed a very powerful transmitter to send BBC overseas broadcasts into enemy territory. Here too, BSC came to the rescue when it was able to obtain the Aspidistra radio transmitter which, with an RF output of 600kW, was the most powerful then available. It derived its named from the

opportune to leak sensational disclosures to American newspaper editors. The day after France fell to German troops, on June 26, 1940, Westrick attended a celebration dinner at the Waldorf Astoria and told pro-German guests that Britain would fall within three months. It had two unpredictable consequences.

Widespread belief in that possibility among German supporters across America reached Roosevelt who, convinced that they could be correct, began to exert pressure on the US Army Air Corps to plan for an intercontinental bomber which could strike Germany from the North American continent. Thus began the requirement resulting in the long-range, B-36 heavy bomber. The second consequence was to accelerate Stephenson's efforts to discredit Westrick by leaking stories about his connections to the Nazi leadership and how he was personally profiting from rumour-mongering and setting one American against another. Westrick returned to Germany in August 1940 and became disillusioned

with the Nazi regime, even supporting an assassination attempt on Hitler, but he continued to represent ITT in that country.

SOFTLY, SOFTLY

Increasingly, the BSC operation operated as a 'gentlemen's SOE' in the United States, working with Hoover, sometimes reluctantly, to find and expose German agents working against American business interests and for the advantage of the Nazi regime. It set up a base at the Princess Hotel just outside the town of Hamilton, Bermuda. There, 1,200 personnel intercepted and analysed physical mail together with telephone and telegraph traffic flowing between America and Europe, disclosing a network of German and Italian spies working through family members who were already citizens of the United States. This was also a conduit for German spies to obtain information about Britain and to use America's neutrality to infiltrate British businesses operating in the USA.

In the opening year of the war there was considerable dialogue and visits from

ABOVE: A memorial to William Stephenson, head of the BSC spy operation, in Winnipeg, Canada, the town where he was born. (David Nyhoff)

ABOVE: US communication companies played a major role in developing coding machines, including the IBM Rockex, adapted as a one-time cypher and precursor to the post-war computers. (Matt Crypto)

popular song by Gracie Fields, 'The Biggest Aspidistra in the World', after the oversize plant favoured in English homes.

Built for RCA in America, it became redundant to use when the Federal Communications Commission placed a maximum 50kW limit on radio transmitters to increase competition for more stations over a given geographic area. The British bought it for $165,000 and it was set up at King's Standing near Crowborough in the Ashdown Forest, East Sussex, as a medium-wave transmitter. Over time it was joined by other equipment, including additional medium-wave and some short-wave transmitters together with a couple of 250kW Doherty transmitters which could be bootstrapped to produce a 500kW output on one frequency. In 1943 General Electric provided two 100kW transmitters which remained in operation through the 1980s. Radio broadcasts into Europe were joined by a BBC long-wave transmitter set up in the village of Ottringham outside Hull.

The remit of the BSC began to expand and in 1941 it was tasked with conducting counter-intelligence and counter-smuggling activity between Italy and Rio de Janeiro to which city the airline LATI had provided a trans-Atlantic service from Rome. The scheduled route provided a conduit for diamonds and platinum and for industrial goods such as mica, which the British wanted to stop, as well as the agents it was pouring into South America. Encouraged by Germany to make good on its promises to use connections to foster good relations with the Axis powers, Italy put considerable resources into influencing foreign policy in countries where it had established connections.

LATI was connected to the Brazilian President, Getulio Vargas, and on the basis that any sabotage operation would be ineffective, a forged letter was 'leaked' purporting to be from the airline's head office containing disparaging comments about Vargas and claiming it was in discussions with the political opposition party. The airline's office in Brazil was shut down and flights stopped in December 1941. In 1942 the country switched sides and declared war on Germany and Italy. BSC had played a vital role in cutting off one of Germany's supporters, halting a leaking border, and blocking an entry point for agents from Berlin and Rome.

ABOVE: Signals intelligence played a large part in winning World War Two and formalised the use of coding machines for communications traffic. (US Army Signal Corps)

ABOVE: Recognised for her ground breaking work at Arlington Hall decoding Japanese messages, Ann Caracristi is at extreme right. (US Army)

BLACK AND WHITE

While the BSC conducted 'black' propaganda among its many activities, the British Information Services (BIS) carried out 'white' propaganda by broadcasting and distributing information supporting the British cause. After December 1941 it received the full backing of the Roosevelt government, many of whose officials, staffers and bureaucrats knew nothing about the work of the BSC. Formed in 1941 by the Foreign and Commonwealth Office, the BIS grew and expanded its operations, eventually operating in more than 40 countries and working with British embassies to further relations, trade, and cultural exchanges in what many regarded as another 'softly-softly' approach providing advantage to the country long after the end of World War Two.

Agents working for the BSC were drawn from many walks of life, notable figures in the post-war world being operatives in the nation's greatest hour of need. In their time, both Roald Dahl and C S Forrester, novelists, and writers of international acclaim, operated as agents for the secret services and for the BSC in particular. After graduating as a fighter pilot with the RAF, Dahl was injured in the Greek campaign, invalided to England and by chance, after meeting the Secretary of State for Air Major Harold Balfour, in 1942 was assigned to Washington DC as Assistant Air Attaché. Offended by the lavish lifestyle in the US compared to the slaughter and devastation which he had lately experienced, Dahl sought a more direct involvement to aid the British war effort.

Unimpressed by the indulgences of British diplomats, including Lord Halifax, who had been placed in America as the British Ambassador by Churchill, Dahl befriended C S Forester who wanted to write his story as an example of the British 'can-do' wartime spirit. Through this connection, Dahl came to know of the work of the BSC and met Stephenson, who quickly recruited him to work against the 'America First' isolationist group who made speeches and wrote pamphlets extolling Americans to keep out of the war in Europe.

Dahl's personable skills were put to other uses, including getting to know Roosevelt's inner circle and keeping Churchill briefed on the President's underlying motivations, while also appraising the Prime Minister of attempts by certain groups at subverting American commitments. Forester worked for the British Ministry of Information and Ian Fleming operated one of the cells reporting directly to Stephenson, all of whom worked with the blessing of Roosevelt to help keep the American people on a sustained course to work for the liberation of countries occupied by Germany, Italy, and Japan. It was an entrenched relationship which would continue after the war and be sustained through transatlantic alliances, defence pacts and intelligence operations.

Today, commentators and opinion-shapers frequently downplay the United Kingdom's role in the world, denying the reality of British influence fostered through several centuries of contact via trading companies and overseas possessions, honed by diplomatic activity through war and peace. In reality, organisations such as the British Information Service provided connections and a degree of influence matched by no other country. Wartime expediency had forged a necessity for the BSC to exist, but it was the BIS and the very British use of soft power which would extend the country's influence and value long after the end of the conflict in which it was formed. So much so that those contacts, and even broader connections through several centuries of trade, influence, and negotiation, are sought by foreign powers around the world today.

ABOVE: A bronze bust of Ian Fleming, part of the British spy network in America before it entered the war, and author of the James Bond novels.
(Fortheloveofknowledge/Wikimedia)

RED FLAG FLYING

When Vladimir Lenin made the fateful train journey from Zurich, Switzerland, to Petrograd (St Petersburg) via Germany, Sweden, and Finland in April 1917, few could have known that he would take charge of a socialist revolution already under way, transform Russia and change the world forever. Ruled for centuries by autocrats, dictatorships in all but name under an all controlling Tsar, unrest and revolution had broken out over the appalling catastrophe of Russia's war against Germany for which in 1914 it had mobilised a largely illiterate people to fight for a country with which it was generally unfamiliar in places it had never heard of.

Social unrest preceded Russia's participation in World War One by several decades and when war broke out, its 166 million population were 95% peasants and diverse in ethnic origin, culture, and language. In less than three years of war, 1.8 million Russian soldiers and 1.5 million civilians were killed, by far the highest casualties of any of the belligerent powers. Torn by poverty, famine and conflict and blighted by an unforgiving environment, radicals and revolutionaries fed an appetite for change, but the revolution brought by several disparate groups, each seeking superiority over the others, failed to gain universal support.

Subscribing to the view that imperialist forces fuelled by capitalism would only be overcome through the actions of the proletariat – collectively, the working classes – as prescribed by Karl Marx, Lenin adopted the principle of 'action', rather than the gradual conversion of the middle classes to what he believed to be a just cause, which had been his previously favoured route for change. Returning to a country fomented by strikes, uprisings, revolutionary councils and violent protests against Tsarist officials, Lenin was adopted as the leader of the Bolshevik revolution by eliminating opposition through violent means and uncompromising atrocities to further the cause he believed would transform Russia into a unified state, a communist country.

Through violent struggles with Poland, battles with White Russians fighting in support of the aristocratic elites and socially privileged minority classes, the toppling and assassination of Tsar Nicholas II and his family and the establishment of the Soviet Socialist Republic (SSR), Lenin and his followers seized total control of Russia. Opposition was fierce and not solely among the former ruling classes, as each political organ competed with the Bolsheviks, some seeking to establish a parliamentary democracy to administer the nation. But Lenin persisted in action rather than persuasion and, on December 5, 1917, the Council of People's Commissars appointed Felix Dzerzhinsky to head the first Bolshevik secret police organisation known as the Cheka.

Much of the story about the Cheka involves its suppression of dissident views, elimination by assassination of anti-communist operatives, and the murder of those considered a threat to the Bolshevik

ABOVE: Idealised in this painting by Isaac Brodskiy, Lenin added fuel to a revolution that had already broken out in Russia when he arrived back in his native country in 1917. (Isaac Brodskiy)

ABOVE: Civil War broke out across Russia with a volunteer army of White Russians fighting the Bolsheviks. (Grondijs, Lodewijk Hermen)

cause. Historians are uncertain as to the number deliberately killed by the Cheka between 1917 and 1922, infamously known as the years of the Red Terror. It is certain that at least 55,000 were killed but the number may be far higher as the national census failed to discriminate between those killed by war or political purges. Suffice to say that the methods were highly successful, eliminating all but the most ineffective and compromised attempts at counter-revolution.

Lenin was obsessed with threats from internal organisations and by capitalist countries who he saw as seeking to overthrow the new regime for political, economic, and ideological reasons. The Cheka quickly developed practices of seeking out dissidents, conducting torture, carrying out assassinations and blocking anti-communist propaganda fed from outside sources. Signed on March 3, 1918, the Treaty of Brest-Litovsk ended the fighting between Russia and the Central Powers of Germany and Austria-Hungary.

Freed from fighting on two opposing fronts, German forces were repositioned to the Western Front and to the Middle East where the Kaiser nursed aspirations of a significant post-war trade in goods and materials. The Berlin-to-Baghdad railway was part of a dream that, by creating a continuous rail route from the North Sea port at Hamburg direct to trading ports on the Persian Gulf coast, he could expand the German empire and challenge British plans for the Middle East while reducing the influence of the Ottoman Empire, now Turkey.

Lenin knew that there were powerful agencies and organisations which would use trade, the strength of international banks, and the increasing wealth and economic

ABOVE: The territories under contest during the Russian Civil War, with Bolshevik secret police and spies suppressing opposition across contested areas. (Hoodinski, Wikimedia)

ABOVE: Felix Dzerzhinsky was the founding head of the Cheka, Russia's secret police and spy organisation, precursor to the KGB and today's FSB. (Novosti)

influence of the United States to destabilise the socialist system in Russia. Very quickly, Russia's Cheka became the centre, and archetypical model for a global spy network working to sabotage counter-revolutionary activities around the world, to subvert democratic rule in major countries, and work for the collapse of the capitalist system.

MOSCOW

While Lenin moved the centre of government from Petrograd to Moscow and set up his office in the Kremlin fortress, debate ensued over preferred ways to convert the world to communism – through inciting revolution abroad or by working covertly to bring about the collapse of capitalist countries. This controversy split the leadership, Lenin becoming increasingly opposed to the rising star, Josef Stalin, who advocated tightening controls on the various socialist organisations operating across the vast expanses of Russia.

On December 28, 1922, its civil war against the White Russians and supporting forces from Britain, the United States, and other participants over, the Russian, Transcaucasian, Ukrainian, and Belorussian Socialist Republics met to agree on the formation of the Union of Soviet Socialist Republics (USSR), from which date all these geographic regions became part of the Soviet Union, the Transcaucasian countries being modern Georgia, Armenia, and Azerbaijan. After a series of strokes which eventually left him speechless, Lenin died on January 21, 1924, his place taken shortly thereafter by Stalin, who would reshape the USSR into a major industrial nation but preside over a state redefined as an instrument of terror, genocide, and murder on a colossal scale.

Before the formalisation of the USSR as a single-state nation of several separate countries, on February 6, 1922, the State

Political Directorate had been formed, the first intelligence service and state security organisation of the new communist government. Its name would change but its function was to conduct espionage and spy activity as an integral part of the state apparatus and be responsible for internal security, foreign intelligence and for the assassination of foreign nationals posing a danger to the Soviet state. It was part of the general disassembly of the Tsarist police, whose members were either recruited or shot – mostly the latter – and who formed the core against which all other government departments were subject for security clearances.

Under the designation NKVD, the interior ministry of the Soviet Union operated from the outset as an agent for organising change in other countries and it quickly began to acquire other organs of the USSR, including the OGPU, or secret police. During the 1930s it carried out purges and organised extrajudicial executions, usually within minutes of summary judgement by an NKVD official, or on occasion by block verdict on a group of people. Responsible too for the great purges of the mid to late 1930s, it conducted genocide in several areas to carry out political decisions made in the Kremlin and, as such, was the task force for carrying out decisions by the leadership. It set up the system of Gulags and conducted brutal administration of those camps, most of which were located in remote regions of Siberia and northern Russia.

Recognition abroad of the new Bolshevik rule over Russia came gradually over time,

ABOVE: The emblem of the NKVD, active in torture, assassination, burglary, espionage and counter-intelligence operations between 1917 and 1930. (Novosti)

ABOVE: A poster calling for a continuation of the Red Terror and the effort of the Cheka to root out dissident political opinion. (Author's archive)

but not before a political cost in many Western countries. In Britain, worker's unions and labour groups that formed the Labour Party in 1900 favoured the shift from autocratic control by a privileged class to a democratic system where each individual had a vote in electing a national government. But the brutal force which accompanied the violent seizure of power in Russia split opinion over how that had been achieved and pro-capitalist voices were raised in opposition to the rising tide of both liberal and socialist causes. All of that played into the hands of more traditional, conservative factions whose voices were raised in protest at the violent upheaval to property and life in communist Russia.

Nevertheless, the Labour Party won the January 1924 general election, giving Britain its first socialist government, albeit a parliamentary minority under Ramsey MacDonald which suffered a no-confidence vote on October 8. Concerned at the rise in support for what it claimed was a slide toward Soviet-style communism, on October 25, 1924, four days before a national election, the Daily Mail newspaper published a letter it claimed had been written by Grigory Zinoviev, a senior figure in the Communist International, and others including Arthur MacManus, a leading future in the formation of the British Communist Party.

In that letter the signatories appeared to support a revolution, urging communist supporters to rise up against the establishment and topple the British ruling class. The ensuing election on October 29 returned the Conservative Party to power with a majority of 63 seats, sweeping aside the Liberal vote and relegating Labour as the main opposition party in Parliament for the next several decades. There is little evidence that the letter was primarily responsible for toppling the Labour government, but it played a part and was an early success story for anti-Bolshevik activists.

The Zinoviev letter was a forgery and historians have sought its author(s) ever since. There was no 'smoking gun' and candidates have been lined up to scrutiny but without result. Circumstantial evidence points to Desmond Morton, a former army officer during the 1914-18 war, and a member of Section V at MI6 from 1919 where he worked on counter-Bolshevism. Morton moved to the War Office in the year of that election and would provide Churchill with intelligence information during the 1930s when he was out of power. Morton was a strong anti-communist and helped shape Churchill's own concerns about threats from Moscow.

ACTIVE MEASURES

The Zinoviev letter was a fake and probably did more harm than good to the anti-Bolshevik cause in that it's unravelling as a forgery foretold of panic and insecurity in establishment appraisal of public opinion. It was this aspect that encouraged Moscow to keep up the pressure on democratic and capitalistic countries, using its increasing array of spy agencies to sow discontent and disrupt the status-quo by inciting reaction from capitalists. From the earliest days of its activity in securing the borders of the newly emergent Soviet Union and clearing out any political opposition, Moscow's security services turned their efforts to supporting pro-communist groups in other countries.

Following the human and economic devastation of the 1914-18 war, by the early 1920s the United States was unquestionably the dominant economic power and the Bolsheviks readily connected with sympathisers, in particular the Communist Party of the United States of America (CPUSA) which immediately after the war had split from the Socialist Party of America to support the Leninist revolution in its call

ABOVE: Fearing communist infiltration of democratic parties in Britain, the *Daily Mail* published a letter purportedly sent by Grigory Zinoviev but rebutted by Christian Rakovsky (right). (Author's collection)

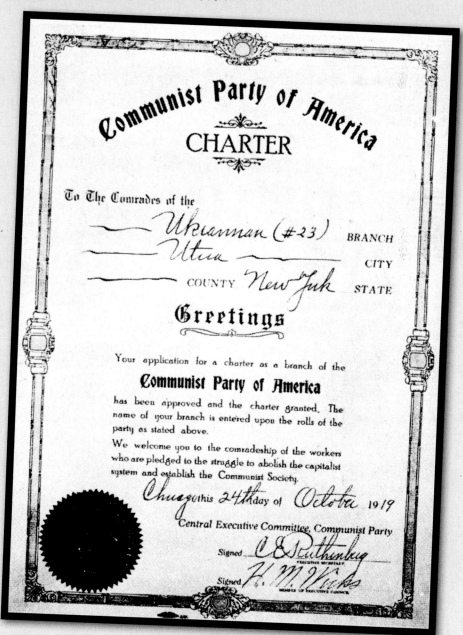

ABOVE AND RIGHT: The badge and charter for the Communist Party of the United States of America (CPUSA) which attracted interest from the FBI and its director, J Edgar Hoover. (Author's collection)

ABOVE: Bookshops selling communist literature were not uncommon across America, this one in New York City.
(Library of Congress)

which were defined as conducting spying, sabotage, assassination, and political propaganda in countries of interest. It is a concept and interpretation of role which began in the early 1920s and continued throughout the Cold War and is a part of Russian activity today. The Russian state apparatus will hunt down and eliminate defectors, counter-intelligence operatives, and activists working against the mother-country and seeking refuge in foreign countries. Active measures also include propaganda and selective discrediting of individuals and agencies working against Russian interests.

Unique to Russia, active measures were non-discriminatory, in that they were applied both within the state and outside its national borders and this became an integral part of espionage training classes from the early days of the Cheka to the spy networks operated by Russia today. In recent years, former Soviet-era active measures have been introduced into the espionage training programmes of other communist states such as China and North Korea.

from a global revolution to establish its own view of a socialist state. The CPUSA worked through the democratic process of labour unions and protest movements, calling for transformation through the ballot box, but Moscow was impatient.

When the US government normalised relations with the USSR in 1933 it opened the door on Soviet spies, prompting a surge in counterespionage activity. With trade and business opportunities feeding the industrialisation of the communist state under Stalin, there were numerous opportunities for Russian representatives to visit America, using the opportunity to make connections with sympathetic organisations such as labour unions and to begin the process of seating 'illegals' in most states.

Illegals are immigrants settling in a foreign country as ordinary citizens but with the purpose of inveigling themselves into society to obtain jobs which provide access to information of interest to a foreign power. The mass immigration policies of the United States during the interwar years set a precedent for more organised and increasingly sophisticated operations of this type, which continued to expand during the Cold War, and which still exists today. Under the guise of international cooperation, technicians, engineers, scientists, and skilled workers began to settle in America for the specific purpose of operating as spies, a secondary group to 'sleepers' who embed themselves in a foreign country to carry out sabotage and guerrilla activity in the event of war.

At first, beginning in the 1920s, Russian intelligence operations focused on obtaining technical information to feed Stalin's programme of massive industrialisation. It ran parallel to the policy of 'active measures'

ABOVE: The Soviet-American trading company Amtorg had its headquarters at this address on Fifth Avenue, a rare example of capitalist opportunism with Russia. (Beyond My Ken/Wikipedia)

ABOVE: Armand Hammer starred as Russia's largest commercial trading partner during the 1930s, proving that business transcends politics. (FDR Presidential Library)

Both of those countries operate on the basis of passive-intervention, where leaked information to national media outlets distribute subversive messages couched in sympathetic tones aligned with the allegiances of the specific print or digital media involved. Thus, can a seemingly innocuous story contain embedded within it undetected and subversive texts known as 'counter-messages', stitching together elements of misinformation and disinformation to hide bias and proclaim objectivity. The training given to Russian and Chinese agents recruited for media interventions favours the passive-acceptance of laudable messages carrying disruptive information, usually untruths difficult to decipher as being false counter-messages.

THE CO-OP

All these practices were developed from techniques used to some extent by the Tsarist police seeking revolutionaries and saboteurs but honed to perfection over several decades of Soviet rule. A further application was to destabilise the internal politics of foreign countries which, perhaps surprisingly, included the United States from the outset. Moreover, to work outside America to several connections between the USA and friendly countries, to discredit the United States as a useful or committed ally, or to show it as working in self-interest rather than through altruistic motives. This became a powerful tool during the 1930s and matured to highly sophisticated practices during the Cold War. As described later, it is a high priority technique used in the Ukraine-Russia war today.

Trade itself became a weapon for political and ideological warfare and in 1924 the Russians set up the Amtorg Trading Corporation, which was in fact the US arm of the All Russian Co-operative Society set up in Great Britain, also supported by the Cooperative Wholesale Society, or 'Co-op', which marketed groceries and goods on a commercial basis with dividends for signed-up members and funds going to unions. Amtorg set up its US headquarters at 165 Broadway, New York and would occupy 261 Fifth Avenue New York, from 1929 to 1941. Controlled directly from Moscow through the Soviet People's Commissariat for Foreign Trade, it handled all goods exported from the United States to the Soviet Union.

Amtorg was not a conduit for spying and espionage, but it was held to high value by the Soviets for its role in allowing Russian trade and currency transfers on a large scale, the explosion in spying and espionage activity only getting underway in the United States when a Soviet Embassy was opened in 1933. A more discreet function was carried out by Armand Hammer, an American businessman and entrepreneur who met Lenin in 1921 and set up a manufacturing operation in return for laundering money diverted to communist organisations across the United States and Europe. Hammer received unique support for his work, which included assistance with moving art collections from the former Tsar's palaces and other notable places across to the US. Hammer's activities attracted the attention of the FBI, who suspected him of espionage, but he was never arrested or charged with any crimes.

Throughout the 1930s, the CPUSA continued to operate and to collect and pass on useful information under its leader, Earl Browder, who worked with J Peters to pass documents and files to NKVD agent Iskhak Akhmerov, living in America under a false identity since 1935. Most useful to Moscow was the Main Intelligence Directorate, otherwise known as Soviet military intelligence, or GRU, which would remain a mainstay of acquiring foreign intelligence to the end of the Cold War and which was succeeded by a similar unit in May 1992. The GRU recruited personnel with a scientific or technical background so that they could communicate knowledgably with scientists and engineers they contrived to meet in foreign countries.

A major spy ring in the United States was organised and run by Ukrainian-born Jacob Golos, a revolutionary who fled from Russia and reached America in 1909 where he eventually joined the CPUSA. While living in the United States he was put in charge of the NKVD's operation there, becoming an authenticated member of the spy organisation. Golos set up a travel company which organised movement for Soviet agents in and out the country and provided fake identities and false passports. When CPUSA boss Earl Browder was arrested and imprisoned in 1940, Golos took over many of his duties, including controlling and handling his agents, before he died of heart failure in 1943.

Golos' lover, Elizabeth Bentley, an American NKVD operative with the codename UMITSA ('good girl') who specialised in putting moles into government jobs and infiltrating the Office of Strategic Services, took over his activities. She combined her expanding activity with an operation run by Victor Perlo, who had his own network for putting communists into positions with the War Production Board and even the US Senate. Falling out with her Soviet masters, Bentley became depressed and sought release through a confession to the FBI in 1945, during which she helped disclose a large network operating in the United States, much of which was brought down by her testimony with 150 people named. Bentley died in 1963 after abdominal surgery.

Active measures had profited the Soviet Union by placing operatives in America on a scale not fully understood until testimony from Bentley and other defectors revealed the breadth and depth of the Soviet spy rings, many turncoats perhaps seeking absolution from their nefarious activities by admitting complicity which had attempted to bleed the US dry of its state secrets. A lot of which involved obtaining information about weapons, policy and plans for everything from the development of more efficient energy distribution to how to build better cars, aircraft, ships, and tanks.

It is a mistake to attribute all Soviet interwar spy activities to attempted political manipulation or subversion of the state. Stalin was intrigued by the way the United States had emerged as the leading economic power and, operating in a vacuum created by Russia's appallingly low levels of literacy and technical abilities, he sought all possible means of industrialising the Soviet Union. He achieved that with the construction of iron and steel works at Magnetogorsk, the second largest city in Russia, modelled after the industrial towns of Gary, Indiana, and Pittsburgh, Pennsylvania following a Soviet visit to Cleveland, Ohio, in 1928 to discuss plans with a US consulting company.

ABOVE: Elizabeth Bentley worked for the NKVD as a Soviet spy in the United States who turned in 1945 and disclosed the names of 150 Russians agents operating in America. (Library of Congress)

A FIGHT FOR MINDS

Revealed by former NKVD operative Elizabeth Bentley, information about the sophistication of Soviet spy rings in the United States came as a shock to many in the Roosevelt government. The FBI had been aware of political activity from the CPUSA and its supporters in Russia and some operatives had been arrested and prosecuted, although Embassy staff had diplomatic immunity. These 'legals' operated on a different basis to the 'illegals' embedded in American society, a group which remained hidden and undetected. However, when Germany invaded Russia in June 1941 the Soviet Union became an ally and relations changed almost overnight.

Only the previous month, Gaik Ovakimian, the senior NKVD operative who had been running the Golos spy ring for a while, was arrested by the FBI for

violating the mandatory foreign registration list. As a gesture of goodwill to its new allies, Ovakimian was allowed to return to Moscow and in May 1942, the President commuted Earl Browder's sentence. But the FBI remained vigilant, and the Army Signals Security Agency (SSA) investigated ways in which it could monitor traffic between Soviet officials working in America. Due to the new relationship, a large number of Russians were now legitimately visiting the US to discuss cooperation on matters relating to the defeat of Nazi Germany.

Under a special arrangement with the FBI, the SSA was given sole responsibility for monitoring and analysing foreign diplomatic and military cyphers and encrypted messages. Based at Arlington Hall, Virginia, SSA personnel used continuing traffic to conduct research into how they could decode these on a regular basis. Both the army and the navy had studied Russian and Japanese codes and by 1942 were decrypting cables between the Japanese Army general staff and military attaches in Berlin and Helsinki. On orders from Colonel Carter Clarke, chief of the Special Branch of the Army Military Intelligence Service (MIS), the SSA started a programme specifically aimed at decrypting Soviet messages.

And there it might have rested, but for a Virginia schoolteacher recruited to work

ABOVE: In late August 1939, Russia's Molotov (seated) and Germany's von Ribbentrop (behind him) signed a non-aggression pact with a secret codicil allowing Russia to attack Poland and take Finland. (Library of Congress)

ABOVE: During the 1930s, FBI director J Edgar Hoover focused resources on foreign interventions in US politics and advised the government on potential threats from the Soviet Union. (FBI)

at Arlington Hall for the war effort. Gene Gabriel was given the task of working with a few other civilians sorting and collating inbound telegrams from the various communications circuits they monitored. Much of the existing knowledge surrounding these messages came from a select group of Finnish cryptologists and over the following months they were able to categorise them into five distinct types. Around half the messages were defined as 'Trade' and came through the Amtorg Trading Corporation communicating with the Soviet Purchasing Commission, most of which was innocuous and related to the lend-lease deals then being negotiated with the American government.

The Russians were aware that their code books had been found in the Petsamo consulate and an agent informed Moscow that German intelligence was trying to use those to decipher diplomatic messages. Finland, an enemy of Russia after Moscow invaded it on November 30, 1939, joined with Germany when that country attacked Russia on June 22, 1941, both now having a common enemy. Russia was not overly concerned about the code books as they were not much use with one-time pads, two identical sheets of paper in the possession of both the sender and the recipient showing

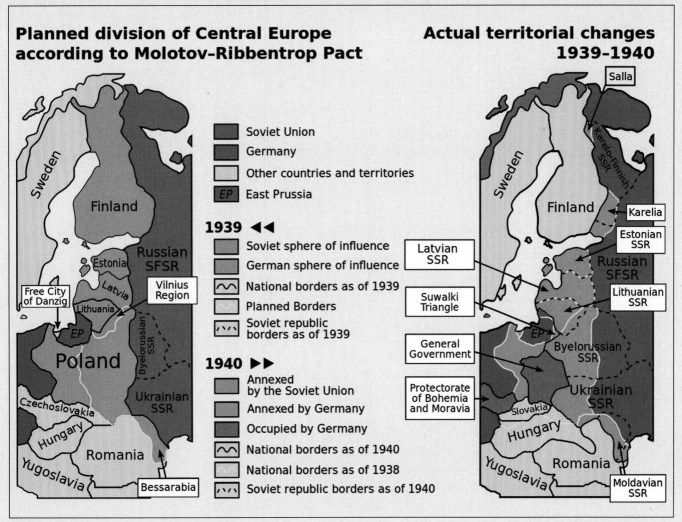

ABOVE: The Ribbentrop-Molotov pact restructured the boundaries of east European countries, prompting a response from US security services to monitor Soviet hegemony. (Peter Hanula)

ABOVE: Pavel Fitin, remembered as the architect of Stalin's foreign intelligence apparatus and the man that warned his boss about German plans to attack Russia. (TASS)

which letters or numbers are displaced from the content of the message so as to write and read it from the same script. In fact, believing them to be unbreakable, the Russians continued to use the same code books until the end of 1943.

CHANGING ALLIANCES

US intelligence agencies were working with a changing set of enemies and allies. The Russians had colluded with the Nazi regime in attacking Poland in September 1939,

which had encouraged the Soviet Union to attack Finland. Considering the Soviet Union as a political enemy, the American government was somewhat at odds with this alliance, but companies trading with Germany took a different view and fell silent on the bizarre relationship between the Nazis and their communist neighbour to the east. However, when Germany turned on its ally and attacked Russia, allegiances changed and created an ally out of a former enemy. America now became an open door for Russian spies, secret agents, illegals, and counter-intelligence operatives.

Throughout this changing period, Moscow had a resolute commitment to use active measures to obtain detailed information on technical and scientific research and on political plans and policies, especially the latter insofar as it related to US commitments to the war against Germany. Four days after the Japanese attack on Pearl Harbor, when Hitler declared war on the United States on December 11, 1941, Moscow sought information held by US intelligence about Berlin's plans for the war against the Soviet Union. Correctly assessing that America had made its own analysis and drawn its own conclusions about German plans, Stalin tasked Soviet intelligence with seeking out that information and Pavel Fitin was given that job.

Chief of the First Directorate of the NKVD, Fitin had rebuilt the foreign intelligence arm after the purges of the late 1930s, reconstructing an efficient and in several respects a better organisation.

ABOVE: A propaganda poster for the US Army Air Corps showing the much lauded Lockheed P-38, details of which the Russians had obtained through their spy agencies. (NARA)

Well informed and perceptive, Fitin gave countless warnings about German intentions to attack Russia before the catastrophic invasion of June 1941, but this was not what Stalin wanted to hear. Falling foul of the controlling Lavrentiy Beria, Stalin's hatchet-man and head of the NKVD, Fitin

ABOVE: Soviet spies sought detailed information on American technology development such as the variable density wind tunnel at the NACA's Langley Research Center. (NACA)

ABOVE: Bruno Pontecorvo worked as a physicist and channelled information to Russia that he obtained while in contact with personnel from the Manhattan atomic bomb project. (Author's archive)

was likely to have been executed for sowing disruptive rumours had it not been for the sudden fury of the German attack he had consistently warned about.

Fitin's primary function had been to obtain information on America's understanding of German war plans, but he also sought that information from informants in London in addition to US and British plans for the overall prosecution of the war against Germany. Throughout, the Russians wanted to know about plans for the invasion of Europe, if only because it would take the pressure off Russian forces fighting on the Eastern Front. Fearing the consequences of a break with declared aims, Fitin was also tasked with determining whether either country was likely to reach a peace deal with the Nazi regime. Stalin was particularly worried that a deal involving German surrender in the west could lead to a resurgent Nazi effort in the east.

Recognising the American advantage in science and technology over Russia's technical programmes, Fitin looked at acquiring as much information as possible about American weapons, munitions, radar, radio devices, and research into the possibility of nuclear bombs. The acquisition of information on these programmes was widespread and not specifically focused on the increasing possibility of building atomic weapons, the concept of which Stalin relegated to the category of 'just another bomb'. Over the duration of the war, Soviet intelligence acquired devices which accelerated production in Russia of many weapons which would be introduced into operational use after the defeat of Germany, including anti-aircraft missiles and a wide range of electronic devices.

PUSHING AN OPEN DOOR

The Russians found the 'open' American society provided easy-pickings in acquiring information which in many other countries would have been almost impossible to obtain. Agents collected vast quantities of trade journals, scientific research papers and general news magazines to keep current with American projects and ambitious government plans. With an open society accountable to the public representatives they elected, citizens were fed information on the basis that they had a right to know how their money was being spent. An alien concept in Soviet society.

In one particular example, aeronautical research funded by the US government was openly available for aircraft manufacturers to exploit in new designs and improved performance. It was that way by congressional law. Set up in 1917, the US National Advisory Committee for Aeronautics (NACA) and the forerunner of NASA, established research programmes in three laboratories studying aerodynamics, wing planform profiles, and aircraft engine

technology. This information and wind tunnel test results obtained, were provided to manufacturers so that they could improve the quality and efficiency of their products and benefit the American economy.

In many other countries, private enterprise was left largely unsupported by government research, and this made the United States an easy target for unscrupulously obtaining the products of publicly funded programmes. The accumulation of material increased as the number of Russian officials in America grew due to the wartime alliance, but the real information they sought was within the lists of proprietary and patent registers which contained manufacturing, detailed design, and innovative designs and technologies.

To cover all these, five major spy networks were set up in America, the largest through the Amtorg headquarters in New York City, and a second net out of the Soviet Embassy in Washington, DC, where officials sought connections with their US counterparts to establish a working relationship for diplomatic purposes. As with most of their endeavours, the Russians failed to discriminate between civil and military activities, blending both into a seamless drive for superiority for the motherland. A third net was set up through the office of the Soviet Consulate General in San Francisco and a fourth was based in Mexico City.

All these were supported by a fifth net operated by Akhmerov, which coordinated activities of the CPUSA and other disparate, socialist-related political organisations in the United States with sympathies for the Soviet Union. The net in Mexico City was operated by Lev Vasilevsky who organised illegals to establish and maintain contact with the Manhattan Project and the development of the atomic bomb. Moscow ordered Vasilevsky to only use illegals in making connections with the atom scientists and to operate those links through Bruno Pontecorvo, the Italo-Russian physicist

ABOVE: Vitali Pavlov (left) persuaded Harry Dexter White (centre) to put Soviet agents in the US Treasury Department in an operation exposed by Whittaker Chambers (right), who was disillusioned by Soviet excesses. (Author's collection/Harry S Truman Library/Library of Congress)

who served as a conduit through which information flowed from the lauded atomic scientist Enrico Fermi and others at the Manhattan Project.

Infiltration and interference became an important part of access to the US government and the Treasury Department was targeted by more than 10 Soviet agents working through sympathisers and collaborators. Much of that used elements of the pro-communist organisations in America, including the CPUSA. In an overt attempt to change US policy toward Japan, while Russia was still an ally of Germany, Vitali Pavlov sought out Harry Dexter White, then the assistant secretary of the Treasury to gain his support for Soviet intelligence operations. In this way he hoped to soften US policy toward Japan and reduce tensions over Japanese action in China. Pavlov claimed Dexter White agreed to place Russian agents in the Treasury to help lower financial pressures that the American government was placing on Tokyo.

A communist sympathiser but disillusioned with Stalin's purges, Whittaker Chambers would testify later that Dexter White's sole function for the spy net was to ensure as many people as possible got into high-level jobs at the Treasury Department. It appears to have worked because another conspirator, Nathan Silvermaster was moved to the Board of Economic Warfare when investigators suspected him of espionage. Dexter White went far beyond his assigned remit and after the war would provide the Soviet authorities with currency plates enabling the Russians to print money which they used to 'buy' American hard goods.

It is difficult not to assess Harry Dexter White as anything other than a wayward pseudo-idealist who was never a committed and dedicated communist but rather a liberal-minded pragmatist who believed his relations with the Soviet Union could be advantageous to the United States in the longer term. It is perhaps ironic that he was a key player in the July 1944 Bretton Woods conference setting up rules, protocols, and the international monetary system which lasts through to the present. Agreed by more than 700 delegates of the 44 allied nations, it came when the defeat of Germany and Japan was virtually inevitable, and the determining factors were to prepare a post-war world in which the sheer magnitude of the Great Depression would be unlikely to occur again.

Not so pragmatic, the communist organisations in the United States were considerably more active than their counterparts had been in Britain and other democratic countries untainted by Nazi occupation or rule by Imperial Japan. But they were left powerless by public opposition to increasingly hostile Soviet belligerence over occupied territories and there were few recruits to support the cause. Disenfranchised by Stalinist atrocities and the realities of Soviet-style socialism, most Americans and the majority of the

BELOW: Russian spies were keen to get as much data as possible and had key contacts at the Bretton Woods economic summit held at the Mount Washington Hotel, New Hampshire. (jbarta/Wikipedia)

British people opted for a more liberal and democratic form of socialism which fuelled a surge in anti-Soviet feeling not long after World War Two.

It was largely as a result of government restrictions and security constraints that the effective use of the American pro-communist organisations lost their value to a central Soviet leadership. That leadership had gained, through almost four years of war, vast tracts of Eastern Europe denied to them at the end of World War One. Outside the Soviet Union, only a few diehards ideologically committed to Marxist-Leninist philosophy remained loyal and an increasing number of turncoats and spies for Moscow were enrolled through greed, opportunism, or both, not a few excited by the danger it brought, but risk with the threat of a fatal outcome as both sides regarded treason as a capital offence.

MOTIVATIONS

In assembling a recruitment plan for spies, many NKVD officials regarded foreign nationals as the perfect magnet for gathering information and as the

ABOVE: Decoders at Arlington Hall working on German and Japanese messages during World War Two. (US Army)

ABOVE: Development of code-breaking activity at Arlington Hall reached a peak toward the end of World War Two and was supported by a college opening on site in 1943. (US Army)

war wound down and a new, post-war world began to emerge, many who believed they were discussing secrets with 'friendly' countries were in reality talking to a disguised Soviet agent. This technique gained traction through international events, scientific meetings where many countries were represented, and organisations were founded for international cooperation. Techniques were adjusted according to the individual approached, GRU agents being particularly adept at 'psyching' out vulnerabilities which could be exploited through social events or sympathetic discourse on world affairs.

This approach reaped many rewards and the use of both NKVD and GRU resources, together with illegals integrating different parties, allowed both social and professional connections to open the door to formal and informal communications between very different groups. In this way, casual and seemingly innocuous conversation allowed Russian agents to glean information they would have found difficult to obtain in any other way. In particular, gossip and general chatter about individuals and organisations added depth to publicly available information in both the political and the corporate world. Industry in particular was exposed to left-leaning union officials

who believed their workers to be victims of greedy capitalists and were only too willing to discuss grievances. Information like this could expose vulnerabilities exploited by apparently sympathetic listeners.

Yet there were a few who deliberately leaked top-level secrets and provided Russia with detailed information out of an apolitical desire to see an equal level of military force, thereby avoiding a world dominated by a single superpower. Paradoxically, many of those who gave the Soviet Union a head start on building weapons of unimaginable destructive power wanted no more than an end to war itself. In that regard, perhaps those primarily responsible for sharing secrets were themselves no more than naive idealists manipulated by those in charge of countries who sought nothing less than the possession of absolute power as a leveraging influence over the affairs of great nations.

As World War Two progressed, and with concerns about Soviet post-war intentions, in 1943 a US counterintelligence operation was set up under the name Venona. It was operated by the Army Signals Intelligence Service and initially assigned to Gene Gabreel, a crypto analyst working for Colonel Carter Clarke at Arlington Hall. Gabreel became the lead analyst and

supported work not dissimilar to that being carried out at Bletchley Park in England where codebreakers sought to decipher messages using Enigma machines. At Arlington Hall, the brilliant crypto-linguist Meredith Gardner reconstructed Soviet code books over several years, establishing a reliable way to translate the messages.

Venona operated until September 30, 1980, and from 1948 involved GCHQ at Cheltenham, England. In its time it discovered that some 200 Americans were operating as agents for the Soviet Union and disclosed a lot more about elements of the British and US secret services involved with the NKVD and other Russian government agencies. It is highly unlikely that Soviet spy Kim Philby, see chapter six, was part of the leak to Moscow telling the Russians that this programme was underway because cooperation with Britain on Venona only began in August 1945. It is certain, however, that Philby was able to verify a leak from William Weisband, an émigré from Russia who became a US citizen in 1938 and joined the Signals Security Agency in 1942 before assignment to Arlington Hall.

As the war ended and Venona began to reveal uncomfortable secrets about the degree to which the Soviet Union had

ABOVE: US codebreakers worked with messages sent on Enigma machines by military units in German-occupied territories. (CmoAGeorgia/Wikipedia)

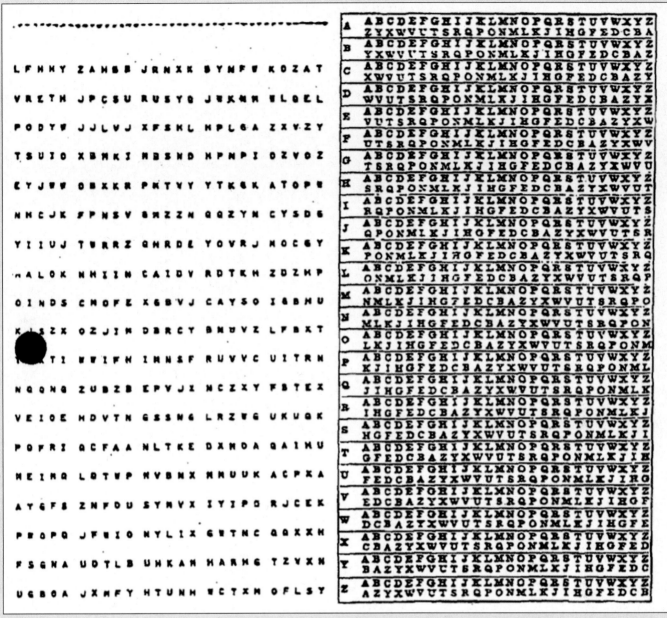

ABOVE: US codebreakers and cypher specialists frequently used the one-time pad, where characters on the key at the left are used to convert the letters on the right into plain text or cypher. (NSA)

penetrated British and American intelligence operations, concerns over leaked secrets began the discussion about the need for more effective internal security clearances. From the President on down, the levels of penetration into every government department had been astonishing, the OSS receiving the greatest number of penetrations and disclosures of any agency. More remarkable was that Venona had been such a closely guarded secret that President Truman was not aware of its existence until 1948 but the British Ultra work at Bletchley Park in Britain had been openly shared with President Roosevelt.

Venona also disclosed that a considerable quantity of information had been obtained through Australian sources, with the Australian Department of External Affairs specifically implicated. The British gained high marks for quickly discovering the paths through which the Russians had established links for obtaining classified

intelligence information but were themselves implicated in significant spy groups. The Americans were shocked at the amount of information leaked through the Australians

ABOVE: Meredith Knox Gardner was a brilliant crypto-linguist who used his skills to reconstruct Soviet code books at Arlington Hall. (NSA)

and imposed restrictions on the level of cooperation with that country. Disclosures embarrassed not only America's allies but raised serious concerns over the security of US organisations and in the post-war period this would attract Congressional committees to begin the process of shutting down cooperation with former allies. In turn, that led to a severing of links which had been so important, and so strong, during the wartime years.

It would take a decade or more for confidence to return because the most disturbing revelations concerned information about the most powerful explosive weapon devised by scientists – the atomic bomb. It was the possibility that British and American spies working for Russia could have significantly accelerated the test of a Soviet bomb that most disturbed the Truman administration and that in itself would change the 'special relationship' between the United States and Britain for several years.

THE CAMBRIDGE FIVE

One of the most infamous episodes in the history of espionage and spy activity at a national level, the recruitment of British graduates at Cambridge University by Soviet special agents has been studied by espionage professionals around the world and is used in classroom sessions at several intelligence organisations in many countries. It is important because it carries many lessons and leaves unexplained the real reason why people betray their country and conduct activity likely to bring down governments and provide political and military advantage to enemy states. The five men named provide a fascinating insight to the world of

the double agent and their controllers. To better understand what motivated them, and to feed those lessons into recruitment helps avert future lapses in deciding what causes such action.

Their betrayal was shocking to the British establishment, not only in the breadth of their infiltration and the extent of the information they provided to the Soviet Union but to the amount of time it took to discover their actions and unravel the complex web of deceit they spun to achieve their objectives over such a long period. Although the first disclosures were known in 1951, it would take a further 39 years for the last of the five to be named, ironically

confirmed by the Soviet double agent Oleg Gordievsky, who defected to the West in 1985 after 11 years of service to MI6.

Collectively known as the Cambridge Five, they probably represent only the most significant in a group possibly much larger and forever hidden by the enveloping sands of time. While today the exploits of the Cambridge Five are public knowledge, their story is more complete and considerably more nuanced than is generally believed. Recruited largely because they preferred the communist system over the capitalist state, and because they distrusted the establishment and believed its institutions to have cronyism at its heart, over time they

BELOW: The appropriately named Mathematical Bridge at Queen's College, Cambridge, a university which fostered intellectual theory together with liberal, socialist and communist groups in the 1930s. (Rafa Esteve)

now recognised to be false. The NKVD was made to look better than it was by the sheer scale of what the Cambridge Five achieved, performing independently and with characteristic British nonchalance and a total disregard for the possibility of immediate disclosure. Made into the stuff of spy movies, books and television series, their audacious and cavalier approach was instrumental in their survival. Analysed in retrospect, it was extraordinary that they endured in their double roles for so long and, through hindsight, the examination of the leaked files and the information they provided cast a poor light on the Moscow Centre, on their controllers and on the NKVD.

The story of the Cambridge Five is a catalogue of individual lives, men following their political convictions practiced through motivations few are called upon to follow. The following capsule biographies highlight very different lives united by a common purpose operating inside a dark and secluded fellowship at variance with both of the opposing organisations that used them. It is perhaps for this reason that they are

interesting, for each honoured a specific purpose unique to that individual, a very exclusive club of different individuals where, in fact, there was no loyalty but only a self-serving life bound within a very personal commitment.

DONALD DUART MACLEAN

Born on May 25, 1913, Donald Maclean was the son of the Liberal politician Sir Donald Maclean, leader of the Opposition between 1918 and 1920, a family with properties in England and the Scottish Borders. The young Donald was educated first at St Ronan's School, Worthing, and then at Gresham's from the age of 13, a school that had produced the noted Marxist military historian Tom Wintringham, the founder of the Communist Party of Great Britain (CPGB). At the age of 18, Donald won a place at Trinity College, Cambridge, where he read modern languages. But the communist message was all around and he fell under the influence of fellow undergraduate James Klugman who reinforced Maclean's growing disregard for

became increasingly effective, both to the astonishment of their handlers and to the Centre in Moscow.

Willing supporters of Soviet-style communism, each had a unique reason for working for the NKVD and were regarded with suspicion by their handlers only because they achieved so much. Because of this, for some time the Russians thought they were likely to be double-agents doing the bidding of MI6 and the information they passed along was frequently subjected to verification by other agents if only to discount the possibility of deliberate deception. It was also checked against probabilities developed by the NKVD itself and on numerous occasions discreet traps were laid so as to expose any double-dealing, yet none of it demonstrated duplicity. They were all true to their adopted cause.

But their disclosure brought concerns to MI5 and a previous assumption that the Soviet secret services were highly efficient is

ABOVE: The Maclean family in 1920 with (left to right) Donald, Ian, Gwendolen and Andrew. (Author's collection)

ABOVE: Coat of Arms for Gresham School in Holt, Norfolk, with the arms of the Company of Fishmongers, where Donald Maclean schooled between 1926 and 1931. (Kolforn/Wikipedia)

recruited by the NKVD with the task of secreting information to his controller. Starting at the Foreign Office in October 1935, Maclean's first job was to work with the department handling the Netherlands, Spain, Portugal and Switzerland and British communications with the League of Nations.

The following year he switched to the Non-Intervention Committee, which monitored countries sending people and materiel to Spain during its civil war and which had its first meeting on September 9, 1936. Throughout this period, Maclean duly provided documents which were photographed and returned to locked drawers at short notice. After a period in which he was seemingly ignored, Maclean was approached by Kitty Harris who acted as a courier between spies and the different Soviet recipient organisations, with the introductory recognition phrase "You hadn't expected to see a lady, had you?", to which he replied, "No but it's a pleasant surprise".

Harris was a 'cut-out', a person who only knew the identity of the person handing over the information and the person she was to hand it to, so as to prevent identities of others in the net who might be disclosed in the event of capture, interrogation or torture. Usually, cut-outs are unaware of where the information ends up, perhaps even which country through which it might pass to avoid identity of the handling organisation or even of its nationhood.

The cut-out break severs the two ends of an information flow and has been used in

the establishment and the capitalist system in general.

Surrounded by fellow advocates of the communist system, Cambridge gave Maclean the environment to flourish, becoming a leading participant in 1934 when he began editing *Silver Crescent*, Trinity's student magazine. There, he could express his allegiance to the Marxist doctrine. During this period, he expressed support for setting a stronger political tone at Cambridge University, commenting on

the decline he saw in rearmament and global trade, on the need for student participation in politics and for the equality of women in all aspects of education and life in general.

In 1932 Maclean had taken a trip to Moscow and this came up when he was applying for a job with the diplomatic service two years later, where he was asked for his opinion of communism, since his earlier support had been in favour of that system. Declaring that he was "disenchanted with it", in reality Maclean had just been

BELOW: The front court to Trinity Hall, Cambridge, where Maclean attended from 1932 to 1936. (Trinity College, Cambridge University)

ABOVE: Much debate at Cambridge University surrounded the rise of Benito Mussolini's fascist party in Italy and the rise of Nazism in Germany. (Author's collection)

the commercial world in recent years, where consultants are hired by intermediaries – the cut-out – so as to prevent biased contamination of data and analysis, ensuring the most objective judgement on the part of the provider. It is now used in the digital world and in computer programmes to hide identities and is the functional core of the 'dark web'.

In intelligence circles, cut-outs deny opportunities for questioning the informant about the identity of the end user. There are cases where the cut-out is taken out of the link and the provider intentionally discloses his or her identity. In such cases, a level of dialogue ensues in which the controller discusses needs and wants directly with the informant, debating what is possible and what is not possible to obtain in support of a specific requirement. These discussions are rare because direct meetings or communications could disclose a network through identification of the end user and that is a point of vulnerability intelligence organisations are loathe to expose themselves to.

There is no indication that Maclean was engaged directly with the end of the line in Moscow but his controller asked him to seek a position with the British Embassy in Paris, where he became Third Secretary on September 24, 1938. A willing servant of the cause, Maclean was guided in his career choices by requests from his controller seeking opportunities to infiltrate different

departments. He became involved with talks between British, French and Soviet diplomats for a possible alliance against the territorial ambitions of Hitler, reporting these to Moscow as well as attempts by France to extricate it from security pledges to East European countries.

Maclean began a relationship with Melinda Marling, the daughter of American oil executive, and when she became pregnant he married her on June 10, 1940, fleeing the

ABOVE: Donald Maclean forged a friendship with Guy Burgess which saw them both defect to the Soviet Union. (UPI)

country together with the British diplomatic staff as the Germans closed in on Paris. For much of the war Maclean worked at the Foreign Office before he was promoted to Second Secretary at the British Embassy in Washington DC, where he arrived on May 6, 1944, and a promotion to First Secretary four years later. Residing in the liberal conurbation of Georgetown, Maclean built a reputation for hard work and professional commitment, success moving him up to a policy committee working the deal between Britain, the United States and Canada regarding nuclear materials.

It was here that Maclean provided the Russians with a comprehensive description of the size of the atom bomb programme, the quantity of materials required for production and the number of atomic bombs that could be built with these resources. Maclean managed to get into the appropriate positions to obtain the most sought-after information required by the Russians, providing detailed statistics on the quantities of plutonium available to the bomb builders. These diverse contacts allowed Maclean to also provide detailed information on aviation, military bases and post-war plans for the US armed services during the period of force contraction and downsizing of land, sea and air forces.

The information Maclean passed to the Russians in this period were the most valuable of any leaked to the NKVD by any British or American agent and while his

ABOVE: Maclean received the Order of the Red Banner of Labour after arriving in Russia where he lived on and off from 1951. (Novosti)

fame is not as great as other spies of his time, it is possible that he did the most damage. Information on a wide range of military and political discussions and decisions were handed to the Russians, files with details of strategic resources and the negotiations leading to the formation of NATO being provided. Maclean took up a post in Cairo in 1948, where he continued to pass details of Middle Eastern policy at a time when the British government was working to establish a post-war influence in the region and where the Russians too were eager to attract interest from local rulers and national leaders.

The pressure of his double life brought stress to Maclean and he began to drink to excess, was sometimes violent with his fists and in his language at social gatherings. Believing him to be mentally unhinged by the pressures of work, these outbursts were used by his wife, perhaps as a contrivance, to ask for him to be returned to London where, after a brief respite, he was promoted to lead the American desk at the Foreign Office. Unknown to him at the time, the Americans were homing in on his double life through the Venona messages, which provided information on discussions between Russian officials abroad and their parent organisations in Moscow.

It was in 1948 that Yuri Modin became Maclean's controller, who later received from his British informant the highly

classified communications between President Truman and Prime Minister Atlee covering discussions about using the atomic bomb. The use of the bomb against China had been requested by Gen Douglas MacArthur in the opening weeks of the Korean War, which broke out in June 1950. Guy Burgess, another of the Cambridge Five and working in league with Kim Philby, was aware that the net was closing in on Maclean and intentionally got three speeding tickets so that he could be sent back to London where he would warn Maclean that he needed to escape.

Confiding about the risks to Melinda, Modin got her approval and set in motion an escape route for Maclean. On May 25, 1951, after saying goodbye to his wife and accompanied by Burgess, Maclean took the ferry from Southampton to France and vanished. Not until 1956 would Premier Khrushchev publicly admit that both men were in Moscow, a city in which Maclean prospered, received a doctorate and settled in to a respectable and comfortable life. Accepted and well-liked by Muscovites, he was joined by his wife and children in 1952. Maclean died of pneumonia on March 6, 1983, remembered in Russia for his work with the Soviet Foreign Ministry in the years since his arrival.

GUY BURGESS

Closely connected with Donald Maclean and one of the most important of the Cambridge Five, Guy Burgess was born into an upper middle-class family on April 16, 1911, and educated at Eton, the Royal Naval College, Dartmouth, and Trinity College, Cambridge, where he arrived in October 1930. His friends and associates there were on the left of the political spectrum, specifically Kim Philby and Anthony Blunt. Joining the University theatre community, he designed stage sets for a production of a Bernard Shaw play in which Michael Redgrave played a leading role.

A self-proclaimed homosexual, Burgess was fascinated by fellow student Jim Lees, there on a mining trade's union scholarship with a very different perspective on life, class and social structures. Socially integrated almost to a fault, Burgess displayed energy and exuberance for all aspects of life at Cambridge and was enthusiastically welcomed into different groups and into the highly intellectual think-tank, the Apostles, entry to which was ensured by Blunt. Burgess was impressed by alternatives to capitalism introduced to him by Lees and by the apparent ease and simplicity of the communist concept of equality and the writings of Karl Marx in particular.

Ignoring his studies to pursue contact with likeminded groups, Burgess failed to get his degree from Cambridge but returned in 1933 as a postgraduate researcher into revolutionary 17th century England and to work as a teaching assistant. Together with

Donald, in November 1933 he marched against the Remembrance Day celebrations in Cambridge, both men believing the national event to be a militaristic and imperialistic glorification of war. Three months later, the two radicals met participants in the National Hunger March on its way through the city and, realising that an academic career was beyond his reach, distractions drew him to Moscow on a two-month visit in June 1934 where he became impressed by the communist system in practice.

Russia's drive to sign up British students from Cambridge University as agents of the Soviet Union was in the hands of NKVD agent Arnold Deutsch, who met Philby in June 1934 and through whom he engaged with Maclean and then Burgess before Blunt and Cairncross in that order. Gripped by a new zeal, and convinced he had at last found his true purpose in life, Burgess prepared himself for some sort of government work, openly professing to denounce communism and distancing himself from revolutionary causes.

For a while he was assistant to John Macnamara, a Conservative MP to the right of his party, and both men joined the Anglo-German Friendship organisation where Burgess obtained details of German foreign policy, duly passed along to his controller. Reconnecting with former friends at Oxford, he applied for a job at the University but was turned down. After twice being rejected by the BBC, in July 1936 he was given a job there as producer for a talk show where he frequently asked Blunt to participate as well as unsuccessfully seeking out Churchill, whom he had met socially, for an interview. Throughout, candidates for invitation were selected by the NKVD controller seeking interviews that could reveal vulnerabilities.

ABOVE: A close friend of Maclean, Guy Burgess followed a similar path, bringing a very different and evocative personality to the spy ring. (UPI)

ABOVE: Burgess attended Eton College, first in 1924 and again for three years from 1927. (Martin Kraft)

Burgess fell out with the BBC when he objected to what he believed to be subservience to the government of the day over objections from the Prime Minister's office to a range of people he had wanted to get on the programme and in November 1938 he resigned. After inveigling his way into consideration for employment with MI6, when war broke out Burgess gained a position with Section D using his previous experience to discuss with the BBC how best to conduct foreign broadcasts opposing the Nazi regime. He was joined by Philby, whom he had brought in to Section D, and both went to STS 17 Brickendonbury to train SOE saboteurs, instruction being made up as they went along as there was no precedent for this activity. While Philby went to a special SOE training camp at Beaulieu, Burgess was dismissed from the service after a drink-driving charge.

Burgess managed to get his old job back at the BBC and after Germany attacked Russia in June 1941 he was tasked with presenting the Soviet Union in a favourable light, now an ally of the British war effort. Using Blunt for introductions, he got NKVD agent Ernst Henri on the talk show and in October he was given control of the

BBC current affairs programme *The Week in Westminster*, opening doors to the political elites of the day. In seeking participants for his programme, Burgess gained access to a wide range of politicians through lunches and social occasions, using his guile to obtain details useful to the Soviet appetite for information on everybody.

From early 1941 Burgess left his flat in Chester Square, where he had lived for six years, and moved in with Blunt at 5 Bentick Street, London, soon the centre of meetings, social gatherings, dinner groups and long conversations deep into the night. Throughout this period Burgess maintained his informal work for MI6 but, forever mindful that he could be exposed at any time, he tried to persuade his handlers that they should assassinate Goronwy Rees, who had befriended Burgess at an Oxford social event in 1932. Burgess had disclosed his work for the NKVD to Rees when he unsuccessfully tried to recruit him in 1937. Rees was now serving with the Royal Welch Fusiliers, a potential threat to Burgess, but the Russians declined the suggestion of a killing.

In 1944 Burgess left the BBC and joined the news department at the Foreign Office,

providing much information to Moscow that helped shape Soviet attitudes at the Yalta conference in March 1945. In what was probably the most damaging to relations with the Russians, Burgess told them of Churchill's *Operation Unthinkable*, a contingency plan to attack the Soviet Union with atom bombs. That plan had been rejected by the senior military leadership as both unworkable and highly undesirable but the very thought of that mindset did damage to how Stalin judged the British.

After the 1945 general election, Burgess grew closer to the ruling Labour government and became private secretary to Hector McNeil, soon deputy to the Foreign Secretary, Ernest Bevin. McNeil was no communist but trusted Burgess, who managed to photograph more than 2,000 pages of policy and strategy files for his controller. For a few weeks in 1948, Burgess was assigned to the Research Department, which worked to counter Soviet propaganda, but his cavalier, distracting and loose lifestyle offended many and he was returned to McNeil, whom he accompanied to Brussels in March 1948 for the signing of the treaty which would begin the lengthy process toward cooperation and union across the continent.

It is uncertain just how much influence Burgess had but when he was sent to China in late 1948 at the peak of the civil war, in which the communists would take control of the country, he may have played a significant role in getting the British government to recognise the new government in 1949. Back in London, he had a boisterous episode with fellow drinkers at a London club and fell down stairs, receiving severe head injuries warranting a spate in hospital. After which he was notably changed, according to Harold Nicolson who mourned the demise

ABOVE: Burgess in 1935 at the time he came under the influence of NKVD agent Arnold Deutsch who led a concerted effort to recruit students for infiltration to the upper levels of the British establishment. (Keystone, USA)

of "…one of the most rapid and active minds I know".

Perhaps surprisingly, given that it is a top-tier posting in the civil service, the Foreign Office sent Burgess to Washington DC in July 1950 as Second Secretary, at a time when Philby was already there running MI6 operations across America. Ideally placed to obtain classified information about America's activity in the Korean War, Burgess supplied his Soviet handler with copious information. Seeming to lead a charmed life, he was given responsibility for looking after Anthony Eden when he visited the United States in November as deputy leader of the Conservative Party.

Called to account for further indiscretions, it was at this point that Burgess 'arranged' to be returned to England so that he could alert Maclean to imminent disclosure and on May 7, 1951, he was back in the UK. As noted in the account of his co-conspirator, Burgess accompanied Maclean when he fled to Russia and began a new life in the Soviet Union. Over time, Burgess became a popular figure and received many visitors, including members of the Labour Party intrigued by his excessive and wayward life rather than for any political connection.

Some believed that while Maclean had probably done the most damage to British foreign relations, Burgess was the glue that united the Cambridge Five but his reckless and unhealthy life style took

LEFT: With access to influential people, Burgess hosted a BBC radio programme from Old Broadcasting House, London. (Andrew Davidson)

BELOW: Together with commemorative plaque, the house in Samara, Russia, where Guy Burgess lived between 1952 and 1955. (Apetrov9703/Eikipedia)

ABOVE: The Church of St John the Baptist at West Meon, Hampshire, where the ashes of Guy Burgess are interred. (Hassocks5489/Wikipedia)

its toll and he died on October 5, 1963. Many testified to his unwavering belief that British and American imperialism had done considerable damage and that the Soviet Union was the only available solution to hegemony and war. The flight of Burgess and Maclean, both men idealists to the end, brought an end to the complacency in the British secret services that had made the Cambridge Five possible.

KIM PHILBY

Archetypical of this group was the enigmatic Kim Philby, born on January 1, 1912 in India and educated in Britain, receiving a scholarship to Trinity College, Cambridge, where he came under the influence of pro-communist sympathisers. After graduating in economics, Philby went to Austria to help victims of Nazi Germany and acted as a courier between Vienna and Prague. He married Litzi Friedmann, a communist who fled with him to England in 1934 after an uprising which pitted communists against fascist sympathisers.

In London, a friend of Friedmann was the likely connection to a Soviet agent operating under the name of Arnold Deutsch who recruited Philby, now working as a journalist for the *World Review of Reviews* and then for the *Anglo-Russian Trade Gazette*, which changed its focus to covering trade with Germany. Under this new focus, Philby made attempts to contact the Ambassador to Britain, Joachim von Ribbentrop and joined the Anglo-German Fellowship, an organisation working to improve relations between the two countries. When he went to Spain in 1937 to report on the civil war

there, Philby began one of the more bizarre involvements, working for both the NKVD and MI6, each receiving his commitment to the ignorance of his involvement with the other.

When Philby returned to London in 1939 his involvement with the Russians stopped for a while and after the outbreak of war with Germany he began working for MI6 Section D, a department looking to subvert Nazi intentions through non-military means. That came via an introduction from Guy Burgess, then

СОВЕТСКИЙ РАЗВЕДЧИК

КИМ ФИЛБИ
1912—1988
5 к ПОЧТА СССР 1990

ABOVE: Remembered on a Soviet postage stamp, Kim Philby was continuously under suspicion after he defected to Russia in 1963. (RIA)

working for the Russians while penetrating MI6 and employed at the BBC, which is when Philby reacquainted himself with the NKVD. Philby certainly had an interesting war. Department D took him and Burgess to run a training course for saboteurs at Brickendonbury Manor in Hertfordshire. It was during this time that Burgess was arrested for drunk driving while Philby was moved to a school for SOE operatives at the Beaulieu Estate in Hampshire.

The Russians regarded Philby as a valuable asset and in early 1941 the London NKVD operative Ivan Chichayev contacted him to obtain information on British agents which he suspected were being trained to operate in Russia, which at this time was still an ally of Germany. Philby professed that no British saboteurs were being trained for that but shared with Chichayev the intelligence reports known to MI6 that Germany was planning an imminent attack on Russia. Other strands of intelligence to that effect were leaked to Soviet agents but Stalin refused to accept the reports, very few NKVD agents having the affront to contradict Stalin's own conclusions, not least his henchman Beria who channelled NKVD information to the Kremlin.

Three months after the German attack on Russia in June 1941, Philby informed his agent that Japan would attack countries in Southeast Asia and not the Soviet Union as Hitler had requested, a message which was endorsed by Richard Sorge, a German journalist spying for the Russians but operating from a base in Japan. In October 1941 Sorge was exposed by Japan's intelligence agency and tortured before

ABOVE: The Russian cypher clerk at the Soviet Embassy in Ottawa, Canada, Igor Gouzenko lived in the apartment at upper right and spied for the Russians but was interrogated by Philby. (I Padraic Ryan)

being sentenced to death, carried out by hanging in November 1944. Sorge's story is a forgotten side of the war involving Germany's attack on Russia, Japan's attack south six months later and unsuccessful attempts by Hitler to get a coordinated attack on the Soviet Union by his Axis ally.

In September 1941 Philby was moved to Section Five which, was responsible for offensive counterintelligence operations, where he dealt mainly with operatives in Madrid, Gibraltar, Lisbon and Tangier, successfully thwarting a German attempt at monitoring the arrival and departure of merchant shipping. In time he was promoted to deputy head of Section Five. Because Russia was now an ally of Britain and America in its struggle to liberate itself from German occupation, MI6 shared

ABOVE: The German journalist Richard Sorge provided the Russians with detailed information he obtained while operating from Japan. (Bundesarchiv)

information with the GRU over German activities in Bulgaria and Romania but the NKVD believed that information was being withheld and complained to the British controller in Moscow, Cecil Barclay. This was conveyed to London and Philby was compromised in a way that gave concern that he was misleading the Russians and working for MI6 as a double-agent.

An even greater possibility of exposure occurred in August 1945 when Istanbul NKVD agent Konstantin Volkov sought political asylum in Britain in exchange for £27,500 and the names of 250 Russian agents working in London and 314 in Turkey. Philby was sent to Istanbul by MI6 to secure the deal with Volkov but, fearing that he could be exposed, he tipped off his Soviet contact and by the time he arrived three weeks later Volkov had been spirited away to Moscow, heavily bandaged from rough treatment and bundled into a Russian aircraft. There is no further record of his fate. Much later, it was discovered that the two British diplomats he promised to name were Guy Burgess and Donald Maclean, not Philby.

Much of the work at Section D had been breaking German codes but that shifted to Soviet espionage activities and in 1944 Philby had told the Russians about Britain's success in cracking cyphers. This came at the time Lauchlin Currie, an American at the White House but an agent working for the Russians, told the NKVD that US codebreakers were about to do the same thing. But the cooperation was about to end, the Russians having obtained more intelligence information about their opponents, albeit wartime allies, than any other country in history. But the Russians

were not the only beneficiaries of this clandestine activity.

Philby continued to impress the senior leadership and several thought that he was destined to become director-general of MI6. But his close encounters with disclosure as a Russian agent were not over. On September 5, 1945, Igor Gouzenko, a cypher clerk at the Soviet Embassy in Ottawa, Canada, walked out of the building, hidden around his person a great collection of files and paper sheets revealing classified activities he and his colleagues had worked on. He wanted to defect but before he could secure freedom he fled, as when Russian security agents discovered the missing files and

ABOVE: Kim Philby made it to Russia in 1963 but the KGB feared that he would return to England and inform on his former masters. (Author's archive)

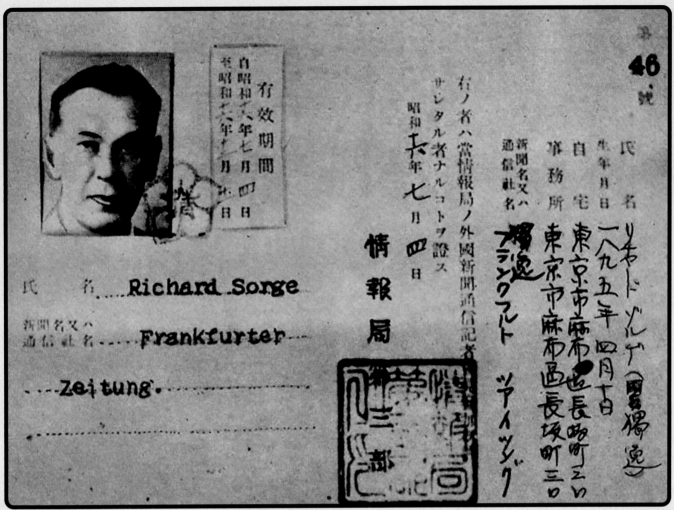

氏名
リチャード（國獨逸
生年月日 一八九五年四月四日
自宅 東京市麻布区長坂町三ノ
勤務所 東京市麻布区長坂町三ノ
新聞名又ハ
通信社名 獨逸 フランクフルト
ツァイツング

有効期間
自昭和六年七月四日
至昭和六年七月
日

有ノ者ハ當情報局ノ外國新聞通信記者
サレタル者ナルコトヲ證ス
昭和六年七月四日
情報局

46號

氏 名 ......Richard Sorge

新聞名又ハ
通信社名 ......Frankfurter

......Zeitung.

ABOVE: The press-pass for Richard Sorge who verified what Philby told the Russians, that the Japanese would not attack Russia. (Author's collection)

pursued him into the night. Gouzenko wanted to buy his new life by disclosing spy rings involving British traitors, which could have included Philby.

The most obvious person to conduct the Gouzenko interrogation was former MI5 investigator Jane Archer who would have been available had she not been moved to MI6 Section Nine of which Philby had been appointed head in late 1944, a position he had manoeuvred himself into at the behest of his Russian handler. With Archer out of the way, Philby was able to deflect attention from himself. In 1940, Archer had come upon reference to a young British journalist, purportedly working for the Russians, which had been Philby, who conducted the Gouzenko investigation along with Roger Hollis, head of F Division (counter-subversion) and a future Director-General of MI5.

In 1947 Philby was sent to Istanbul as First Secretary at the British consulate and, as such, in charge of intelligence operations where he was involved in legitimate work trying to get émigrés acting as British agents into Soviet-controlled Armenia and Georgia but that failed. Two years later, Philby was assigned to Washington DC as First Secretary and ran US intelligence operations for the secret service. But Venona revealed the names of US spies and cast suspicion that there were British agents working for Russia, disclosures which coincided with the arrival of Burgess in 1950, who went to live with Philby and his wife. With contrived reasons for being expelled from America, Burgess went back to the UK and Philby warned him by teletype over the imminent threat of disclosure but when he and Maclean fled the country further suspicion fell on Philby.

Suspicion rumbled on and following intensive interrogation by MI5 he professed his innocence and avoided dismissal by resigning from MI6 in July 1951 to take up several journalistic jobs. These gave him cover for some clandestine work for MI6, initially in Beirut and then across the Middle East. By this time Stalin had died and the former government structures were changed, the NKVD being dissolved and reactivated as the KGB. When their agent Anatoliy Golitsyn defected to America in 1961 and told the CIA about double-agents, fearing the worst, Philby vanished on January 23, 1963, and got to Moscow where he was placed under close supervision as the Russian's feared that he would return to England and tell all he knew about Soviet networks.

Philby spent his time working on active measures, rewording official US documents and material to insert false words, phrases and sentences to imply a malicious intent. Denied the full recognition he felt he deserved and never given the rank of colonel which he had understood would be his, he died of heart failure on May 11, 1988. Ironically, Philby had been protected by the British establishment, unwilling to raise a scandal, and he had been tolerated at MI6 due to the inability of the system at the time to accept that a person of his background and education would serve against the interests of his country. Much was to change over the years ahead.

ABOVE: Suspected of informing the Russians about codebreaking progress in the US government, Lauchlin Currie was never prosecuted. (US State Department)

ANTHONY BLUNT

Highly cultured and connected in the highest places within the British establishment, a recruiter for the NKVD and a spy for Moscow, Anthony Blunt certainly helped Russia in the war with Germany but the amount of damage he did to national security is open to debate. In that regard, he is one of the more enigmatic characters among the Cambridge Five.

Born in Bournemouth to a vicar and his wife on September 26, 1907, he moved with his family to France when his father became a member of the British Embassy chapel in Paris, where he devoured the cultural history of that country and became a lifelong student of the arts. Educated at Marlborough School in Wiltshire, while there Blunt started a magazine discussing political matters and receiving contributors from the political left. Gaining a scholarship to Trinity College, Cambridge, he studied art before switching to languages, graduating in 1930 and becoming a Fellow of the college two years later.

Travelling across continental Europe in pursuit of his studies, Blunt made no secret of his homosexuality, a dangerous admission at the time, and had become a member of the Cambridge Apostles, 12 of the self-defined intellectually superior undergraduates. Blunt gathered around him others of similar disposition of whom a considerable number were Marxists, Cambridge probably having the highest percentage of communists in the country, a rich recruiting ground for both undergraduates and graduates. As a Fellow, Blunt travelled to Russia in 1933 and the following year may have been recruited to the NKVD although the exact date is uncertain. Being the more senior, it was possibly through Blunt that several other,

ABOVE: Anthony Blunt informed for the Russians during his time working on Ultra, codebreaking for MI5 while giving the NKVD details of German operations.
(University of British Columbia Library)

unnamed supporters, were brought into the fold of informants. But it was through Burgess that Blunt met Arnold Deutsch, the NKVD handler who schooled him into recommending other candidates and may have been crucial to Philby, Maclean and Cairncross joining the group of spies.

On the outbreak of World War Two, when Germany attacked Poland in September 1939, Blunt joined the British Army and was one of those evacuated by boat from the shores of Dunkirk. In that year of 1940, he joined MI5 and worked on Ultra intelligence from decrypted Enigma messages and while at Bletchley Park he met and recruited John Cairncross to work for the NKVD. Blunt sent

numerous messages and copied documented materials for the Russians, perhaps even operating as the cut-out for Cairncross, although that is uncertain.

Blunt provided highly valued material to the NKVD, including details about Nazi undercover operations in Russia and in that regard assisted an ally, while passing information which very few knew existed. Uncompromising, Blunt believed that the Russians should have been given the Ultra secrets from the time they were attacked but that ran counter to restrictions placed as a result of suspicion about long-term Soviet intentions. Many, including Philby, agreed with that and openly spoke of their contempt for 'politicking' while an ally was under attack, perhaps ignoring the fact that Stalin was committed to bringing down the established order in Western democracies.

Succeeding Kenneth Clarke to the post, after the war Blunt became Surveyor of the King's Pictures but suspicion followed him and many knew of his sympathies for the communist regime, his presence within high society and influential elements of the establishment restraining full exposure. However, when Burgess and Maclean fled to Russia, Blunt fell under closer investigation and in 1963 he was identified by MI5 as having spied for the Russians. He confessed to that in confidence on April 23, 1964, and the Queen was informed.

The public would only become aware of his actions when he was named in the House of Commons by Prime Minister Thatcher on November 15, 1979, after which he was stripped of a knighthood he had received in 1956 for services to art. Dishonoured and stripped of his honorariums, Blunt died of a heart attack on March 26, 1983.

ABOVE: Blunt attended Marlborough College in Wiltshire, England, seen here with its diverse architectural styles. (Dabble/Wikipedia)

JOHN CAIRNCROSS

A fellow conspirator to Anthony Blunt, in providing the Soviet Union with details and decoded messages about German plans during their war with Russia, John Cairncross was born on July 25, 1913, in Lesmahagow, Scotland. Educated first at a local school and then Glasgow University, Cairncross attended the Sorbonne in Paris and Cambridge University, studying languages. Employed at the Foreign Office, he leaned toward socialism and around 1936 joined the Communist Party of Great Britain. Stiff and prickly by nature, Cairncross was recruited as a spy by James Klugmann from that organisation and in 1942 was assigned to Bletchley Park working on deciphering Ultra messages about German operations in the Soviet Union.

Securing a place working at Bletchley Park had been at the behest of his NKVD controller, along with a request for specific information, a not unfamiliar requirement of spies working for the Russian secret services. German field commanders sent messages using the Lorentz rotor-based cypher machines and the Russians were especially interested in the decrypted text in support of battle planning in both offensive and counter-offensive operations. Keen to obtain raw signals in code, the Russians preferred to conduct their own attempts at deciphering the radio messages and Cairncross supplied those too using a separate route. In 1944 he joined MI6 Section Five on counter-intelligence and continued to leak information about those activities.

ABOVE: John Cairncross worked with Anthony Blunt on sending decoded messages to the Soviet Union during the Second World War, working at Bletchley Park from 1942 to 1944. (Author's collection)

ABOVE: Oleg Gordievsky worked for the British as a double agent while serving as the KGB chief in London between 1974 and 1985, revealing countless UK spies working for the Russians. (Author's archive)

Implicated by inference when Burgess and Maclean fled to Russia in 1951, after a full confession in 1952 Cairncross was dismissed from government service without employment or money. His handler, Yuri Modin, helped him move to America where he taught languages at several universities and made a full and open confession in 1964, a year after Philby fled to Russia. The

British authorities considered requesting extradition but the Americans could not find evidence that he had endangered US security and it was not pursued. There is little evidence that Cairncross provided any information of material threat to Britain and after moving to Rome in 1967 to work with the United Nations, he returned to England and died of a stroke on October 8, 1995.

ABOVE: The library at the Sorbonne in Paris where John Cairncross attended after schooling in Glasgow, Scotland. (Zantastik)

STEALING THE ATOM

The British spies known as the Cambridge Five were civil servants given access through employment to classified documents and secret files, passing them to their Soviet handlers because they felt that Marxist-Leninism was the way forward for progressive societies. For them it was primarily a political and ideological choice, although in some cases the element of money eased the decision to betray their country. However, it would be wrong to believe that the five who contravened their voluntary commitment not to reveal what they knew to a foreign power were the only ones involved. At less effective levels, and sometimes in direct support of the Cambridge Five, were friends and associates who either knew of their betrayal or kept their suspicions to themselves. We will never know the full extent of that group, most working in small clusters but some operating individually and largely unaware of the rest.

But there was another group who signed the Official Secrets Act in Britain and were subject to the Espionage Act in the United States, those for whom possession of weapons of mass destruction by one power alone was against their view of a world in balance. They felt it to be immoral that any one country should hold such power over the rest of the world, possibly threatening local wars and the possibility of a globally destructive and catastrophic conflict. These were the atom spies, some of them scientists and engineers working on the design and development of nuclear weapons in the United States.

While those working on the Manhattan Project to produce an American bomb and who leaked secrets to the NKVD did so on the basis of principled and humanitarian concerns, only a tiny minority supported

ABOVE: Unlocking the secrets of nuclear fission would release energy of great magnitude, making it a weapon of enormous destructive potential. (US Army)

ABOVE: Change of shift at the uranium enrichment plant at Oak Ridge, Tennessee, where work into the atom bomb raced at high gear, involving several thousand people as potential security threats. (US Army)

communism and Stalin's Russia. A majority distrusted the United States not to use the bomb for leveraging power in a divided world and sought to balance that by helping the Soviet Union to get their own weapon of mass destruction. Nevertheless, the development of the atomic bomb by a multi-national team of scientists working on the Manhattan Project from 1942 has overshadowed details of how keen the Russian scientists, and others across Europe and in the UK, were to develop their own bomb.

Under the Tsar, in 1910 Russian scientists conducted research into the workings of the atom and a diminished effort continued after the revolution that brought Lenin to power in 1917. During the 1920s and 1930s, British scientists conducted groundbreaking work at the Cavendish Laboratory at Cambridge University in England. Conducted by Ernest Rutherford, research there attracted several international scientists including Russia's Georgi Gamow and Pyotr Kapitsa. In 1934 Gamow fled Russia and went to the United States while Kapitsa would play a major role in the development of physics and the Soviet atom bomb.

During the 1930s, Soviet research on numerous technical and scientific programmes were compromised by Stalin's

purges, which sent many scientists and engineers to the Gulag where they wasted away over years of unproductive activity. The merest indication of dissident thought, talk, or action condemned many intelligent

and capable men and women to the wastes of Siberia, stunting national capabilities and putting Russia several decades behind the West. It was this way with aviation and rocket research, and it prevented the Soviet

ABOVE: The international contribution to the Manhattan Project was significant. The programme director General Leslie Groves converses with British scientist James Chadwick during planning for the atomic bomb. (US Army)

Union from reaping the benefits that could have given Russia the atom bomb and long-range rockets much earlier than achieved in reality.

Neither Stalin nor his Kremlin comrades understood science and they failed to foresee the potential in nuclear physics, repeatedly refusing to give it priority. Elsewhere, physicists were hard at work unravelling the secrets of the atom. In Britain, it was at the Cavendish Laboratory that the neutron was discovered during February 1932 and where the potential of nuclear physics was realised. Progress was rapid across several laboratories in different countries.

In December 1938, Otto Hahn and Fritz Strassmann working in Berlin demonstrated that the atom could be split by bombarding uranium with neutrons and producing barium, proof that an atomic bomb was theoretically possible. That had been discussed in Britain and was also debated through a letter written by Leo Szilard and Eugene Wigner in the United States and endorsed by Albert Einstein, delivered to President Roosevelt in August 1939 imploring him to develop an atomic bomb before the Germans could.

With the Americans not yet in the war, enthusiasm at a political level was only moderate, although some research funding was provided. In Britain, there was greater urgency and Otto Frisch and Rudolf Peierls, refugees from Nazi Germany and carrying out research at the University of Birmingham, calculated that a critical mass of uranium-235 weighing 104lb (47kg) could produce a bomb. Or 22lb (10kg) of plutonium-239 for a different design. The critical mass is defined as the minimum required for a sustained chain

ABOVE: Otto Hahn, who in 1938 with Fritz Strassmann demonstrated that it was possible to split the atom, here with his wife Edith. (Bushmills McCallan)

reaction. Development of both types would be undertaken for America's Manhattan programme.

In Britain, the reporting memorandum on the Frisch/Peierls work dated March 1940 had great persuasive influence and instigated the MAUD Committee, its name being a contrivance from a letter written by the Danish physicist Niels Bohr where he referred to his housekeeper, Maud Ray. Four months later, Britain decided to share with the United States its work on nuclear fission and to discuss with Canada the supply of materials to make that possible. Britain had neither the facilities nor the money to develop a bomb on its own, and considerable investment had already been made in the development of conventional weapons.

The decision to develop the atomic bomb was made in 1941 but officially sanctioned on August 13, 1942, the name Manhattan coming from its first offices in that district of New York. General Leslie Groves was to manage the work and scientific direction was under Robert Oppenheimer, who would manage the scientists, mathematicians, and engineers located at Los Alamos, New Mexico. The work involved 200,000 people across 30 separate facilities in America, Canada, and Britain. Only a few hundred were sufficiently aware of the general nature of the programme and to have been in a position to provide valuable information to a foreign power.

A great many scientists working on the development of the atomic bomb came from Europe, their exodus motivated by the Nazi regime from which they had fled to seek safer lives in Britain and America. Some had relatives already living in the United States harbouring concerns about the rise of fascism in North America. Pro-Nazi organisations had popped up across many European countries on extreme ideological principles dating back to the latter part of the 19th century when racial purity and antisemitism had been rife among some communities. It had spawned similar organisations in the United States, as will be explored later.

THE ATOMIC FIVE

Shared in number with the Cambridge Five, it is entirely coincidental that five prominent names in the development of the atomic bomb were spies sharing details with the Soviet Union: Klaus Fuchs, Bruno Pontecorvo, Alan Nunn May, David Greenglass, and Harry Gold. Leaked information continued to be passed after the

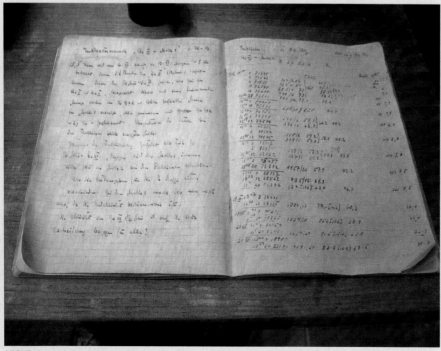

ABOVE: Otto Hahn's notebook in which he recorded his calculations describing how neutrons bombarding uranium could produce barium through fission. (Deutsches Museum)

dropping of the atomic bombs on Hiroshima and Nagasaki in August 1945 and for several years after the end of World War Two. Most spies provided information over a period of time, but one fled the United States and only disclosed classified information after he arrived in Russia. In the following summaries of the parts they played, individuals are listed in the order of the most damage they are believed to have incurred.

Klaus Fuchs

Born in Germany, Klaus Fuchs fled to Britain in 1933, gained doctorates from Bristol and Edinburgh universities and went to the United States as part of the British atomic-energy mission. He lived in New York and worked on a gaseous diffusion plant for U-235 separation, moving to Los Alamos in August 1944 where he remained until June 1946. Back in Britain, he ran the theoretical physics division at Harwell. Fuchs had joined the communist party while in Germany and remained true to his political convictions while feeding the Russians with large quantities of detailed information about weapons work at Los Alamos, in Canada and in the UK.

Fuchs was arrested on espionage charges in February 1950 and given a 14-year prison sentence from which he was released early in 1959 before leaving the UK for communist-controlled East Germany. There he married and spent the rest of his life on scientific research until his death in 1988. Although he may have contributed to China's atomic bomb research programme, the amount of value he provided to Russia is probably more in the detail about American and British plans, providing the NKVD with the largest amount of information they ever received on these

programmes. Under Stalin's henchman and as head of the NKVD, Lavrentiy Beria was in charge of the Soviet bomb project and because he distrusted foreign agents the scientists working on Russia's bomb were given very little of this information.

Bruno Pontecorvo

Italian by birth, Bruno Pontecorvo was educated at Rome and Paris and escaped through Spain to the United States when Germany attacked France in May 1940. Working at first for an oil company, he came into contact with nuclear physicist Enrico Fermi and was invited to work on Tube Alloys, the name of the British-Canadian contribution to the Manhattan Project which he joined in February 1943. Pontecorvo had communist sympathies and was constantly under suspicion by the British and the Canadians, although his work took him to areas of research more closely associated with future projects such as the thermonuclear fusion, or hydrogen, bomb.

After the war, Pontecorvo joined the British Atomic Energy Research Establishment but remained in Canada for the commissioning of the NRX, by far the most powerful research reactor in the world at that time. Gaining British citizenship in February 1948, he moved to the UK in January 1949 and worked on reactor designs at Harwell. In September 1950 he fled to the Soviet Union with his wife and three children, adding to concerns about the information he had already passed over and to that which he held in his head. Pontecorvo had little direct connection with the Manhattan work but a considerable knowledge of post-war plans for bigger and more powerful bombs, of

the materiel which was sought and acquired for that work and of plans for new and improved facilities. He died in September 1993 aged 80 years.

Alan Nunn May

The third of the atomic five, Alan Nunn May was a British scientist who worked at Cambridge University's Cavendish Laboratory from 1942 and moved to Canada the following year to work on the physical challenges of building a bomb. While there he passed laboratory samples of U-235 and U-233 to Lieutenant Angelov, a Russian GRU agent who suffered from radiation poisoning while carrying them to his embassy. A member of the Communist Party since the 1930s, lapsed from 1940 but still a committed ideologue, Nunn May continued to supply information to the GRU and was given the details of a new controller when he returned to London in September 1945.

Nunn May was disclosed after Gouzenko, the cypher clerk in the Ottawa, Canada, defected in late 1945 and revealed the identities of several agents working for Russia, very nearly identifying Philby. Like so many associated with other, Left-leaning, scientists working on the atomic bomb, it appears that Nunn May spied for the Russians because he believed in a world where power was balanced, and that unilateral possession of atomic weapons was less likely to ensure peace. Here again, another early advocate of what would eventually be known as 'mutually assured destruction' to maintain a balance instead of a monopoly.

Nunn May declared to his interrogators that he felt that this was, after all, the reason why so many scientists had fled Germany

ABOVE: The German Klaus Fuchs, one of the 'atomic five' feeding secrets of the Manhattan Project to Russia via NKVD operatives. (National Archives)

ABOVE: Italian-born Bruno Pontecorvo worked on the Manhattan Project and on more advanced weapons after the war, fleeing to the Soviet Union in 1950. (Author's collection)

ABOVE: While employed at the Cavendish Laboratory, Cambridge University, Alan Nunn May obtained uranium samples which he passed to a Soviet GRU agent, exposing Philby after he defected in late 1945. (Author's collection)

to work on an American bomb – so that Hitler would not be the only world leader to have this weapon of extreme destructive power. He also attested to his commitment to the peaceful use of atomic energy and the use of nuclear physics in the development of a nuclear energy supply system for underprivileged countries where resources were limited.

Arrested in March 1946, Nunn May was given 10-years of hard labour but released in 1952. For a while he worked for an instrument company when no science institution would have him, before working in Ghana on a solid-state research programme where he also opened a science museum to encourage local interest. In 1953 he married the former wife of the Austrian physicist and NKVD spy Engelbert Broda. Returning to Britain in 1978 he lived in a small village outside Cambridge, where he died in January 2003.

David Greenglass

Unique among the atomic five, David Greenglass was not a scientist. An American, born in 1922, he was brought up on the lower East Side of New York City, schooled at the Brooklyn Polytechnic Institute and the Pratt Institute. At the age of 16 years, he joined the Young Communist league and became a lifelong supporter of that doctrine. As an army technical sergeant, he was employed as foreman at a Los Alamos machine shop where he prepared apparatus for the Manhattan programme and obtained information far beyond areas he was cleared to access. The pace of the programme left overworked staff rushing to complete security clearances and Greenglass used guile and cunning to gain access to areas which he had no clearance to visit.

In 1942, Greenglass had married Ruth Printz, also a communist sympathiser, and both would pass information to the NKVD. After the war, he teamed

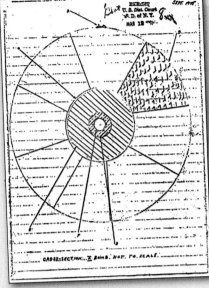

ABOVE: David Greenglass drew this sketch of an implosion bomb which he handed to Julius and Ethel Rosenberg. (FBI)

with fellow conspirator Julius Rosenberg in running a small machine shop in Manhattan but a string of disclosures starting with Klaus Fuchs led to another agent, Harry Gold, and from him to Greenglass and their contacts, the Rosenbergs. It all unravelled and Greenglass was arrested by the FBI in 1950 and in his confession told interrogators about Julius and Ethel Rosenberg. In his remorseful statements, Greenglass described how he had provided detailed engineering information to supplement the scientific details provided by Fuchs, thus revealing a complete package of scientific and engineering detail about the Manhattan programme and how the plutonium and uranium bombs were designed.

Greenglass provided a wide range of information that helped expose the gaps in US security and by providing such copious information pleaded for clemency, his attorney saying that he had, after all, provided more information of value to

improving US security than any damage done by his gifts to the Russians. The judge disagreed and sentenced him to 15 years imprisonment, but he was released in 1960 with a third off in remission. Reunited with his wife, he would later brag to the press that he had lied to implicate others in the hope of a lighter sentence and that he had implicated the Rosenbergs unjustly but that he regretted that, while maintaining a steadfast commitment to what he had done and openly admitting that he would not have changed anything that he did for the Russians. Greenglass died in July 2014, retaining his belief in communism to the end.

Harry Gold

The fifth member of the atomic five, Harry Gold was the most prominent in a group of supporters willing to work as 'donkeys' acting as couriers, intermediaries, recruiters, and messengers between those stealing the secrets and those getting them to the NKVD, sometimes directly to Russian secret service officials themselves. They never were in the same position as those working closely on classified projects, but they knew how to make the connections and play supporting roles without which the transfer of information could never have taken place.

Born in Switzerland in 1910 to Jewish-Russian parents, the American Harry Gold immigrated to the United States in 1914 and was politically influenced toward socialism by the financial crash of 1932. Although he never accepted a friend's invitation to join the Communist Party, in 1940 the NKVD's Jacob Golos recruited him to spy for the Soviet Union, his

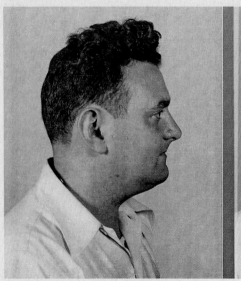

ABOVE: The American David Greenglass obtained information while working for the US Army in a machine shop at Los Alamos and passed secrets to Julius and Ethel Rosenberg. (FBI)

ABOVE: Operating as a courier and a go-between, Harry Gold was never a committed communist party member, but he provided material to the NKVD until exposed by Klaus Fuchs. (NARA)

ABOVE: The Grand Jury viewed the actions of Julius and Ethel Rosenberg as high-level treason, and they were condemned to death in 1953. (FBI)

of the bomb has it that the Russians were disinclined to favour information obtained through foreign spies and that Soviet scientists worked their own experiments independently. Perhaps not understanding this, both Julius and his wife Ethel, the sister of David Greenglass, laboured intensively to obtain the most information they could.

Julius was arrested in July 1950 and testimony from Greenglass implicated Ethel who was arrested the following month. The Grand Jury took a particularly strong view of what the Rosenbergs had done, and both were condemned to death, executions being carried out in June 1953 followed by a large gathering estimated at more than 10,000 to the funeral service held at a Jewish cemetery in Pinelawn, New York.

Many people, including family members, professed his innocence, claiming that his trial and execution were down to national paranoia and that others given prison sentences were far more involved. The trial judge appears to have taken the view that because the Rosenbergs had conspired to extensively recruit spies, they had the greater guilt compared to the atomic five and many more who went to their graves without disclosure.

controller being Semyon Semenov who also handled Ethel and Julius Rosenberg. Gold met Fuchs and operated as a go-between, moving information to his NKVD contact until he was arrested by the FBI in 1950 on evidence from Fuchs. Given a 30-year prison sentence, Gold was released on parole in 1965 and died in 1972 during heart surgery.

COURIERS AND CARRIERS

Frequently included in discussion of the atom bomb spies, Ethel and Julius Rosenberg did irreparable damage to US national security by influencing others into espionage activity. They also provided highly detailed and classified information on a wide range of projects, including electronics, jet engines, jet aircraft and a wide range of technology research projects. Among these were complete blueprints of the Lockheed P-80 jet fighter, but it was to obtain details of theoretical studies and general discussion about work on a fusion bomb that the NKVD asked Julius to recruit Greenglass. Ironically, neither man understood nuclear physics, or the difference between fission and fusion bombs, let alone the value of what they were handing over!

Of the American fission bomb under the Manhattan programme, reports conflict as to the value of the information Rosenberg leaked and to its usefulness on the Russian equivalent, some who worked on the Soviet bomb saying it was a great deal, while others on the project dismiss it as virtually useless. An objective history

ABOVE: General Groves (right) poses with the chief scientist on the Manhattan Project, Robert Oppenheimer at the base of the tower where the first detonation of an atomic device took place at Alamogordo, New Mexico, on July 16, 1945, four years ahead of the Russians. (US Army)

353/24

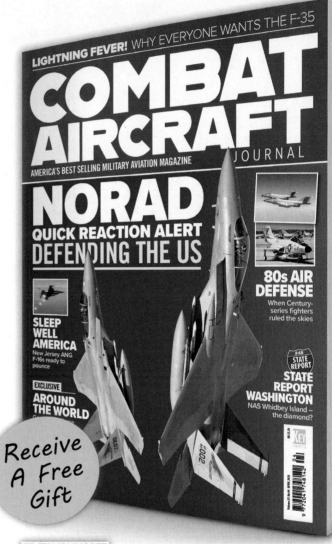

AMERICA'S SPY SHIELD

Nations spy on each other to detect imminent attack, build information on which they can alert their defence networks or obtain intelligence to give them an advantage should war break out. In that context, the individual spy has now become a nation and tools of the trade have grown more advanced than anything used by individual espionage agents. Today, the United States spends almost $100billion a year on its national and defence-related intelligence assets, comprising 18 separate and individually managed government organisations, nine of which are under the Department of Defense. All have undergone considerable change since they were established and most reflect the dramatic evolution in roles, policies and technologies since they were formed.

The oldest of these is the Office of Naval Intelligence (ONI), formed in 1882, which has gone through many changes in structure and role since its formation. Initially set up to evaluate potential maritime threats to America, it monitored developments in Europe as sail gave way to steam and coastal protection forces gave way to blue-water

naval operations in which Britain led the world. After the limited use of maritime power during the American Civil War of 1861-1865, the US Navy fell into decline and not before the turn of the century did it begin to adopt some of the ships and equipment of European maritime powers. Mindful of the blockade set by the British during the Revolutionary War for independence, expanding commercial interests of the United States exposed vulnerabilities which threatened its widening trade with countries around the world.

Responding to rapid industrialisation and expanding commercial enterprises, the former naval officer and President of the United States, Theodore Roosevelt was determined to present his country to the world and establish a global presence, for influence and trade. On December 16, 1907, 18 American warships of decidedly pre-*Dreadnought* design, departed from Hampton Roads, Virginia, sailing around the world, visiting six continents and logging 16,751miles (26,958km) to arrive in San Francisco on May 6, 1908. Known as *The Great White Fleet*, it provided for the ONI a

ABOVE: The Office of Naval Intelligence was set up in 1882 to help protect America's maritime ambitions by securing information about foreign naval capabilities. (ONI)

wide range of detailed information on ports, harbours, estuaries, coastlines and on the naval provisions in foreign countries, while waving the stars and stripes.

When World War One broke out the role of the ONI was expanded to include protection of US coastlines; submarines had entered the naval forces of European

ABOVE: The American warship *Virginia* in San Francisco as it heads the *Great White Fleet* which circumnavigated the world in 1907-1909. (NARA)

belligerents and German ships were in danger of being sunk, perhaps along with neutral American merchantmen. In an extension of its work, it also started tapping into communications and postal services as concern grew that secret agents could be working to undermine naval capabilities. When America entered the war in April 1917, those threats grew more acute and the ONI took on a broader and more engaged form, working with the FBI during the interwar years to maintain a vigil on naval security. During World War Two, in which it became engaged in December 1941, the ONI set up a special department to carry out surveillance of Japanese residents of the West Coast facing the Pacific while simultaneously tapping into telephone calls and mail connecting Japanese families with their relatives.

It was only with the advent of the Cold War in the late 1940s that the ONI began to adopt roles it maintains to this day. Despite the post-war downsizing of the US Navy, the ONI was strengthened, the lesson from Japan's unannounced attack on Pearl Harbor prompting establishment of the Operational Intelligence Section formed in

1946. The role of the ONI was broadened to include criminal activity on facilities as well as monitoring and plotting the movement of Soviet naval forces, such as they were before the mid-1960s when the Cuban Missile Crisis of 1962 forced the Russians to drastically expand their naval capabilities under Admiral Gorshkov.

Because of these developments, the ONI developed the Sound Surveillance System (SOSUS), a series of hydrophones on the sea floor capable of monitoring the movement of passing ships, becoming operational in the 1950s and developing into a sophisticated system for locating Russian submarines through triangulation. In close cooperation with Britain, the ONI developed a system which became the mainstay of Cold War surveillance and monitoring through a hydrophone array covering the seafloor between Greenland, Iceland, the Faroe Islands and Scotland. In this way it was possible under favourable circumstances to log Russian submarines moving from the Arctic Ocean into the North Atlantic. It also provided calibration for monitoring the effectiveness of NATO submarines in achieving stealth and avoiding enemy acoustic arrays.

ABOVE: The naval race set by the British *Dreadnought*-class was joined by all the major sea-faring powers before World War One. (L M Glackens)

After the collapse of the Soviet Union in 1991, naval intelligence underwent a major transformation, moving to new headquarters at Suitland, Maryland, where it co-located with the Coast Guard Intelligence (CGI) unit monitoring domestic maritime activity, and the Marine Corps intelligence units for planning littoral operations. In all cases, knowledge about maritime and naval operations in countries around the world was at the heart of all these activities, with pre-planned contingencies for local and regional emergencies wherever they emerged. Formerly known as the Information Dominance Corps, from 2016 the Information Warfare Community has been assisted by the ONI for linking disciplines and forces for an integrated capability.

BIG BROTHER

Defence-related intelligence information is both universal and highly segmented into individual sectors, such as that generated by an individual, collected through signals, acquired by photographic means or obtained by analysing potential threats from foreign powers or rogue states. Signals intelligence is the business of the US National Security Agency (NSA), one of the largest intelligence-handling government bodies in the world with more than 30,000 employees and an annual budget of about $15billion. It is arguably one of the most important US intelligence organisations, in that it deals with the broadest expanse of signals information which contributes toward the President's Daily Brief (PDB), a report prepared by the CIA.

Set up by President Truman and effective from November 4, 1952, the NSA emerged from the shadows in 1975 when it became public knowledge after a period during which it grew to incorporate roles and duties far removed from its original mandate.

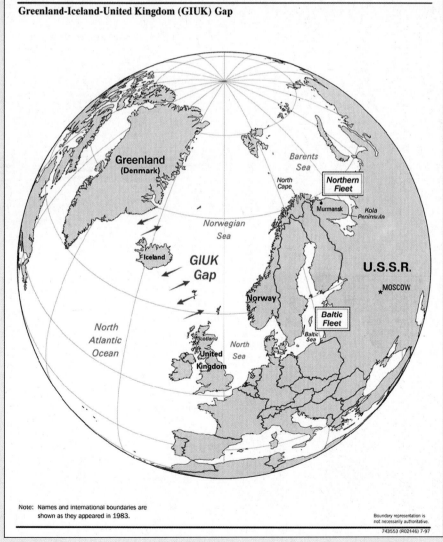

Greenland-Iceland-United Kingdom (GIUK) Gap

Note: Names and international boundaries are shown as they appeared in 1983.

Boundary representation is not necessarily authoritative.

743553 (R02446) 7-97

ABOVE: A sea-floor sound surveillance system covers ship movements in the Greenland-Iceland-UK (GIUK) gap monitoring surface and subsurface movements into the Atlantic Ocean. (CIA)

ABOVE: USNS *Neptune*, a cable repair ship servicing the sea-floor surveillance system connecting communications from hydrophones with shore installations. (US Navy)

Connected through landline, undersea cable and through satellite and cell-phone towers, it monitored foreign communications and that conducted between foreign governments and their embassies and dispersed offices. But it grew to include much more and during the Vietnam War it was directed by the President to eavesdrop on US citizens with support for anti-war movements and others who were connecting with foreign organisations or embassies on a security watch list.

During 1975 the US Congress held a series of hearings to unravel the extent to which the executive branch of the government and the White House were instrumental in using legislative organisations such as the NSA for political or partisan causes. The Watergate scandal, where senior Republican Party officials bugged the offices of the Democratic Party, an event which led to the resignation of President Nixon on August 9, 1974, created broad public concern at the behaviour of elected officials. During interrogations of government officials, the US Congress put the NSA under open scrutiny and provided some assurance of accountability to the general public at large.

It was during those hearings that the House and the Senate learned of a history of wiretaps and the use of bugging devices on US citizens, activity sought at the behest of the White House and by the NSA itself in pursuit of its original goal but somewhat outside the range of activities it was set up to conduct. In response to disclosure about the use of government spy agencies

by the President to monitor opposition politicians and parties for partisan purposes and political gain, Congress passed the Foreign Intelligence Surveillance Act of 1978 controlling the amount of unwarranted eavesdropping on US citizens without cause.

Open acknowledgement that the NSA existed gave it the freedom to explain to the public the value it provided for the security of the United States, obtaining evidence about culprits responsible for atrocities. One example which fed into a justification for the enormous resources applied to the NSA was the signals intelligence obtained after the bombing of a Berlin discotheque on April 5, 1986, which killed two and wounded 79 Americans among a total of three dead and 229 injured. The US government under President Ronald Reagan publicly held

ABOVE: The National Security Agency was established in 1952 to monitor both general and specific threats to the United States at both a military and civilian level. (NSA)

Libya under the rule of Muammar Gaddafi responsible for the attack. The Air Force launched a series of strikes just 10 days after the event which resulted in a number of Libyan Air Force aircraft destroyed at the expense of one US Air Force F-111 fighter-bomber shot down over the Gulf of Sidra with the loss of both crewmembers.

By the end of the Cold War and throughout the early 1990s, some politicians sought to dismantle much of the intelligence structure that had built up during the years of tension between the Soviet Union and the United States and its allies. Others posited the view that in an uncertain world where countries were rebuilding their government structures there was a greater need for signals intelligence than ever before. The NSA took the view that rather than be seen as a spy-hole into the former Soviet Union, it should be regarded as a looking-glass into fast-changing geopolitical challenges, where threats were now multi-faceted and no longer the product of a single superpower.

New technologies began to emerge in this uncertain, post-Cold War world which had direct bearing on the business it conducted and in the role it would play in a future where digital communications and the Internet flourished. Traditionally, collecting signals intelligence required intercepts of radio communication, usually between government departments, agencies or institutions in foreign countries, or from embassies in the United States communicating with their host countries abroad. There was very little direct monitoring of private connections except those linking different departments of commercial companies. With the increased use of cell-phone technology in the early 1980s, radio signals allowed communication on the move without landlines.

The intelligence communities saw this expansion of 'wireless' communication as a unique opportunity for eavesdropping on messages which would otherwise go undetected. Governments applauded the new technology and provided incentives for commercial exploitation, opening up frequencies and bandwidths to encourage everyone to get a pocket-phone. Suddenly, anyone was available for a 'watch list', without their permission and without their knowledge that this was happening. As the World Wide Web (WWW) expanded, the role of the NSA found new value in that the surge in new applications for communications and wireless conversations was in the very sector for which it had been set up in the 1950s, a time when such possibilities were science fiction.

With the advent of electronic mail and file sharing, the telephone became the mainstay of commercial and business enterprise and the attraction of using a national security agency to keep watch on commercial deals between companies trading across boundaries was too great an opportunity to pass up. Quickly, during the 1990s the technology to intercept wireless traffic was thrown back from the national intelligence agencies to corrupt and mischievous operators seeking advantage on all kinds of different deals, from goods to financial services and even to accessing the business arrangements of commercial competitors.

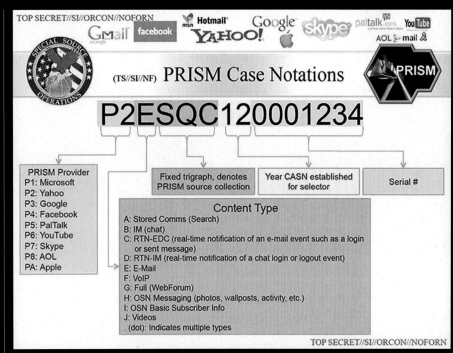

ABOVE: Operating plan of the PRISM programme, extracting information of use from social media platforms including Microsoft and Facebook. (NSA)

ALPHABET SOUP

During the 1990s, the NSA worked the THINTHREAD programme, a highly complex and sophisticated encrypting system for tracing potential villains by scanning email and cell-phone messages to automatically identify threats from several million simultaneous nodes. The danger perceived by some was that individual messages or calls could be decrypted by the NSA and given to agents for identifying the people involved, which was against the law. THINTHREAD incorporated several separate new technologies, including the more effective filtering of several million messages simultaneously, encrypting specific cell-phone numbers for privacy together with an automated auditing system, automatically analysing and identifying multiple contacts for identifying links between individuals plotting activity threatening national security.

Over time, THINTHREAD was replaced with TRAILBLAZER and elements of that were used to develop its successor, TURBULENCE. The enduring database

BELOW: The headquarters of the NSA at Fort Meade, Virginia, an organisation which employs more than 30,000 people. (Trevor Paglen)

ABOVE: On information from the NSA, among other intelligence agencies at home and abroad, President Reagan (right) consults with Congressional leaders and cabinet members prior to the 1986 air strikes on Libya. (White House)

ABOVE: Microwave signals flood the airwaves which are easily intercepted, such as wi-fi payment systems carrying personal and financial information. (HLundguard/Wikipedia)

connections in homes where a voice-actuated signal allows intelligence-activated software to know what is being requested from a cloud-based data bank carrying music, podcasts and any other type of entertainment requested by a human voice. In this way, ordinary people in ordinary homes deliver a vast amount of quality data far beyond that carried on social media channels, simply by turning on their 'smart' devices. Although in reality no one needs to turn them on; that can be done remotely too, effectively turning the 'smart speaker' into a microphone.

Beginning in the 1990s, the NSA worked with industry and academic institutions to develop new algorithms with strong encryption capabilities, work which provided a great range of opportunities for Silicon Valley and for tech giants such as Apple and Google. On the basis that 'if you can't control it, take charge of it', the NSA provided a clear lead so that its core role was tailored to the adaptive and innovative technologies designed by mathematicians, computer scientists and technology builders putting together the new generation of language and digital services which would best serve the interests of the intelligence industry.

The result is a wireless world in which people would be encouraged to carry their lives in a digital device, always accessible to interception, the consequences of which would be a surge in cyber-crime, fraud and disinformation through mass messaging and the innate human susceptibility to mischievous interventions. Encouraged to carry vital information about their most closely guarded possessions, such as bank accounts, credit cards and health information through a keypad on a cell-phone, renders the individual to greater danger of identity fraud and mass phishing activity than would have been possible before the smartphone age. It also opens the possibility of mass-observation on a colossal scale by corrupt organisations.

FEAR FACTORS

But the capability to replace mass-observation with mass-intercepts required a conciliatory public, accepting a loss of

ABOVE: Software manipulation through hardware such as SIM cards and memory systems can 'pair' smartphones and steal access through brushing-techniques, where one phone-carrier passes close by another and captures the link. (Ilya Plekhanov)

throughout is MAINWAY which at its inception was a brilliant piece of integration with existing, large-scale telephone trunks operated by AT&T, Verizon and T-Mobile. From these and others which have since joined the group of commercial providers, the NSA can process main data and communications channels and social network, conducting analysis which can pick off the side lobes of communication packets. Moreover, it can pursue evasive routing plotted by 'dark' callers operating through the Dark Web of overlay networks evading the identity of the source, of the recipient or the message itself.

MAINWAY has the capacity to contain almost 2trillion call-detail records which carry a coded set of information providing the caller and the recipient with GPS location, the time and date, the duration of the call, where it was sent from and to which location it was delivered along with the path taken to connect the two parties. Powerful information which can characterise

the life and style profiles of several billion individuals.

The commercial landline, cell-phone, Internet companies and service providers are paid by the NSA to supply the connections to power MAINWAY and to allow intelligence analytics to access several trillion calls or messaging connections. Nobody sits and listens to these messages. They do not need to because the sifting and filtering allows persons of interest to be identified through their communications footprint, only transferring to a human analyst the identity of those filtered to be of concern for security reasons.

The system was not known to the general public until investigative journalists broke the story in 2006 but the technology has moved on and now embraces a much wider access due to the remorseless desire on the part of the general public for 'smart' devices, each of which does the same as a cell-phone call. It now includes smart-speaker some personal freedoms for greater security and safety from terrorism and rogue players threatening the individual. The trigger for that acceptance was 9/11, the attack on the Twin Towers, New York City, and on the Pentagon on September 11, 2001. The fear this instilled in Americans came from the similarity to Pearl Harbor, when the US naval base at Honolulu was attacked by the Japanese. It instilled a sense of isolation and changed the way the government and the NSA set about responding to what President George W Bush called the War on Terror, when addressing the nation five days after the attacks.

The search for those responsible for 9/11 and the enhanced levels of security required to provide greater assurance that such acts would be prevented, opened a broader and much more intrusive surveillance of the American public, which was at first accepted as the price to pay for security. Some personnel within the intelligence community were unhappy at the level of intrusion into the private lives of US citizens and by inference, those allies cooperatively working with the NSA in a global context. That included GCHQ in the UK, closely integrated with the signals intelligence collected and filtered by both organisations, much of which went through the Five Eyes

group including Canada, Australia and New Zealand in addition to the UK and the US.

The origin of the Five Eyes can be traced back to 1941, the period immediately before America entered World War Two, when British codebreakers at Bletchley Park were cracking Enigma codes used by German military communications and signals units. It was within the liaison established to unlock those messages that a cooperative undertaking resulted in the UKUSA agreement signed on March 5, 1946, which set a special relationship between Britain and the United States, work which would eventually bind efforts between the NSA and GCHQ at Cheltenham, England. Shortly thereafter the other three members of the Five Eyes were admitted and the ECHELON intelligence network became the standard programme for monitoring signals involving military and diplomatic communications within the Soviet Union and the communist bloc.

By the early 1970s, dedicated satellite facilities were being introduced, connecting stations located around the world for securing SIGINT and maintaining a global network of information channels but after 9/11 the pace and intensity of traffic monitoring and handling grew measurably. As discussed in a subsequent section, the

NSA began to switch its attention from potential conflict with Russia to terrorism and to commercial, industrial, political and military growth in China. The Pentagon has for long held concerns about the use of signals and intelligence-gathering in that country and has sought to better quantify the potential threat both in commercial and military terms. This resulted in a tilting of the axis of attention from Europe to Southeast Asia.

In recent years the NSA has come under intense scrutiny, both in the United States and abroad for its alleged contravention of lawful constraints on its activity and on its deep-dive into the lives of ordinary citizens. Some have alleged that its activities extend far beyond either its remit or the legal boundaries that define its role. In many ways it remains an operationally evolved instrument for collecting overseas signals, gathering domestic data within the United States and carrying out hacking activity in the search for terrorists and those conducting subversive activity. Opponents and whistle-blowers accuse the NSA of conducting the very operations they seek to disclose, perhaps missing the point that the agency does not prosecute consequences, merely providing the information that others seek to exploit.

ABOVE: Along with the NSA and intelligence agencies in Australia, Canada and New Zealand, the UK makes its most obvious contribution to the Five Eyes intelligence collective through GCHQ at Cheltenham, England. (Adrian Pingstone)

GATE GUARDIANS – THE STORY OF THE CIA

Hailing itself as the "Nation's first line of defense" and perhaps the most famous of US government spy agencies, the Central Intelligence Agency (CIA) is independent of any affiliated connection to other federal institutions and reports to the President over all matters to do with the security of the country, the safety of its citizens and the national status of the other 194 countries around the world. A very wide range of services are provided by the CIA and many are openly available to anyone, anywhere. Probably the most frequently visited on the Internet is the World Factbook, providing detailed and up to date information about every country. Many Americans use this as a reference file before travelling out of country.

With more than 20,000 employees and a budget in excess of $15billion, the CIA is a civilian agency focused on counterterrorism, counterintelligence, cyber intelligence and on collating a wide range of information gathered from individual agents with signals decoded, messages deciphered and platforms set up to covertly gather data, images and voice traffic. It is primarily concerned with obtaining information about foreign countries and developing analytical tools for interpreting the material it receives and providing analyses to the highly limited group of people to whom it reports. It is not primarily concerned with domestic monitoring, much of that being taken up by the National Security Agency (pages 66-71).

The CIA has its headquarters in Langley, Virginia, and is now named the George Bush Center for Intelligence in recognition of the service provided by that former President of the United States (1989-1993) when he was director of the agency in 1976. In its purpose, the CIA closely matches the objectives of Britain's MI6, from which it harvested much of its responsibilities combining covert and overt intelligence gathering to advise the national leadership about impending threats. It differs in that it has sponsored and developed various technological assets to obtain detailed information from denied areas around the world, specifically the Soviet Union during the Cold War and from unfriendly states since 1990.

But the origin of the CIA can be traced to clandestine British activity in causing disruption across enemy-held territory during World War Two and to the formation

ABOVE: The seal of the Central Intelligence Agency, which was formed in 1947 from wartime intelligence operations and the activities of the Office of Strategic Services (OSS). (CIA)

of the Special Operations Executive set up by Churchill to 'set Europe alight' in areas occupied by German forces. That inspired President Franklin Roosevelt to establish the Office of Strategic Services (OSS) in June 1942 which mirrored the activities of the SOE across Europe and of the Commandos in France and Norway.

ABOVE: The original headquarters building of the CIA during the 1950s. (Author's collection)

ABOVE: The CIA is now located at Langley, Virginia, managing offices in most countries around the world. (Carol M Highsmith)

The use of such forces to obtain intelligence impressed Roosevelt, as did the activities of the British Security Coordination (BSC) operated by the British in the United States to work undercover to bankrupt companies dealing with Nazi Germany (see pages 22-31).

Under President Truman, major changes were to take place as a direct result pf these wartime experiences and the National Security Act set up a train of events which would see the establishment of the CIA on September 18, 1947. The core model upon which it was based came directly from the activities of MI6, the SOE and through experience working alongside the British in Europe and the Asia-Pacific region against enemies of both states in Nazi Germany and Imperial Japan. Which is why the CIA took upon itself a programme of intervention and covert activity, applied to peacetime security concerns.

There was some opposition to the formation of the CIA from the military intelligence organisations and from the FBI, which saw the function of this new body being competitive rather than complementary. But there was an underlying reason why an intelligence organisation capable of connecting both foreign and domestic security surveillance was necessary for complete protection from disruptive operatives connected to foreign governments. And it came from an uncomfortable recognition that pro-Nazi elements in the United States had worked assiduously to overthrow democracy and replace the elected head of state with an autocratic dictator aligned with a foreign power. It was not only the communists that threatened security across America and that had begun during the 1930s.

SWASTIKAS IN THE USA

A few weeks after Hitler became Chancellor of Germany at the end of January 1933, his deputy, Rudolf Hess, instructed Heinz

ABOVE: The headquarters building is known as the George Bush Center for Intelligence, after the former Director of the CIA, George H W Bush. (NARA)

Spanknöbel to form a Nazi party in the United States by merging two existing American organisations supporting Nazi ideology, racial supremacy and eugenics. Known as the Friends of New Germany, on March 19, 1936, it was remodelled into the German American Bund (GAB) with headquarters at 178 East 85th Street in Manhattan, New York, with Fritz Julius Kuhn as its *Bundesfürer*.

Its primary function was to recruit support among ordinary Americans actively campaigning against Jewish groups, communist infiltration, labour unions it accused of funding from Moscow and the liberal administration of President Roosevelt. The Bund had groups across the United States and frequently held rallies and meetings to gather support. Marches were held in major cities and training

camps which were opened to indoctrinate the young into its beliefs. Claiming to restore the fundamental principles of the founding fathers, it even believed that George Washington was the first American fascist who, they claimed, had been an early advocate of its principles.

These displays of extremist political viewpoints offended the vast majority of Americans but Russian sympathisers found the Bund alarmingly aligned with an increasing tide of European fascism in all its varied forms, including the ruling parties in Italy, Germany and Spain. Many pledged commitment to helping the communist cause as a bulwark against what they feared was a rising tide of Nazi support. That appealed to Moscow as a potential battleground for fomenting revolution and Russian spy agencies mobilised its illegals in

ABOVE: President Gerald R Ford meets with the CIA Director, George H W Bush in 1975. (NARA)

Department worked together to break up the Bund. Kuhn was found guilty of embezzlement and sentenced to five years in prison and his successor, Gerhard Kunze, fled to Mexico but was deported back to the United States where he fell under the peacetime military draft of September 1940, the first in US history. Enticing resistance to this law, that required conscription if called upon by the government, Kunze was sentenced to 15 years in prison for espionage. Other members of the organisation were either found guilty of spying or interned for the duration of the war. In 1945 the security services deported Kuhn to Germany.

The presence of the GAB introduced some legal dilemmas in that, to suppress its revolutionary efforts, the FBI and the security services had to spy on American citizens for reasons of political expediency and that introduced a confliction. The FBI could conduct investigations into suspected criminal activity but it had no remit to suppress political opposition. The Bund carefully avoided any illegal activity or any crime but its presence was anathema to the

America to use them to sow fear among the general public. In turn, this got the attention of the FBI and it became an adjunct to the work of the British Security Coordination under Stephenson.

Concerned that confrontation between the two extremist organisations could incite street fights similar to those that had broken out across Germany before the Nazis came to power, the FBI and the New York Police

ABOVE: Concern about national threats to American democracy arose in the United States during the 1930s with the German America Bund, a pro-Nazi organization. (Library of Congress)

ABOVE: The flag of the Bund organization which closely copied the flag of the German Nazi party and was displayed at meetings across the United States. (NARA)

government and to its counter-espionage activities. It ran against the spirit of the constitution and would provide a pivotal point on which legal justification for pursuit of the individual rotated.

While efforts by the FBI to eliminate Soviet agents had a legitimate legal foundation, because they worked for a foreign power to destabilise the government the political freedom for US citizens to campaign for a different government was enshrined within the constitution. That is what the Bund professed to do. Because of that, the American Nazi organisations were tolerated at the margin of legality but their presence, as much as those of the Soviet spies, brought legislation which would make such bodies illegal.

Combined threats from fascist and communist groups prompted the establishment of the House Committee on Un-American Activities on May 26, 1938. This would begin the broader discussion as to security constraints necessary in a democracy and it would open general congressional debate which would allow laws on internment for foreign nationals arriving from countries in which the United States was in conflict. It significantly transformed the way the government, Congress and the security services balanced the need for tighter security on how imported extremist movements were behaving and who was seeking to extract the nation's strategic secrets.

But just how legitimate is it for a government to spy on its own citizens and is that wholly in the national good or a dangerous and slippery slope toward a 'Big Brother' state, prying into the everyday activities of ordinary individuals, or worse? It is a dilemma as ancient as the art of spying itself and has troubled democracies for centuries and it troubled the House Committee on Un-American Activities too. However, when it became a permanent committee in 1945 the

concerns which it had dealt with in preceding years provided the appropriate apolitical environment for a security and intelligence organisation shaped to look both inward and outward, toward those countries who sought to influence affairs in the United States.

There is no direct link between this committee and the formation of the CIA but the discussions which it had ensured that there came into being an agency which connected threats inward to the United States with plots to overthrow the principles of the Constitution and impose autocratic rule. Preparing staff and recruits, the Office of Training and Education was set up in 1950 to prepare personnel for a wide range of field and desk activities according to individual skills and talents. Some would go into field operations overseas, working covertly, while others would develop technical devices and put together

ABOVE: New York District Attorney Thomas Dewey successfully won a conviction against the German America Bund leader Fritz Kuhn. (NARA)

requirements for engineers and scientists to build and operate.

After 9/11 the CIA decided that it needed to improve its educational programmes by creating a career path for recruits and to encourage retention in older employees. This inspired the creation of the CIA University, which is today located in the Dulles Discovery office complex at Chantilly, Virginia. Agents need to be sifted and filtered according to aptitude and schooled in skills essential to carrying out their work, which is frequently conducted through offices close to or run out of US Embassies where station chiefs coordinate activities and ensure safety and essential support. Activities range across a wide spectral range and provide opportunities for personnel to move between sectors, which is encouraged to give agents a wide range of experience and to test personnel for their suitability in different roles.

Choosing the right kind of individual is a skill honed though several decades of experience with a diverse range of applicants. Many are unsuitable, driven perhaps by an inappropriate sense of adventure, a desire to feel rewarded through access to state secrets or an unhealthy attraction to an elevated feeling of importance and power. Psychological analysis of the individual recruit plays a significant role in recruiting personnel, where self-fulfilment, a sense of service to country and a desire to use finely honed skills for complex and difficult work attract high marks. But the recruitment process and procedures for security clearances are a little different from those required for a regular civil service job, where the Diplomatic Security Service has a relatively standard procedure, routinely handling several thousand applications.

Prevailing factors crucial to a successful application for the CIA begin

ABOVE: Texas Democrat Martin Dies Jr as chair of the Special Committee on Un-American Activities which investigated organisations such as the Bund and preceded the permanent committee. (Harris & Ewing/White House)

Am 18. Februar 1943, wenige Wochen nach der Katastrophe von Stalingrad, richtete Dr. Goebbels an eine Massenversammlung im Berliner Sportpalast die Frage:

„Wollt ihr den totalen Krieg?"

Ein begeistertes „Ja" war die Antwort der Nazi-Versammlung. Heute weiss Deutschland, was „totaler Krieg" bedeutet, besser als es Dr. Goebbels und seine Ja-Schreier im Sportpalast voraussahen. Der totale Krieg, den die Nazis wollten, wird mit immer stärkerer Wucht und Wirkung fortgeführt werden, bis Deutschland bedingungslos kapituliert.

DAS DEUTSCHE VOLK MUSS SELBST WÄHLEN:

ENTWEDER Fortsetzung des totalen Nazi-Kriegs bis zur völligen Vernichtung der deutschen Arbeitskraft und Industrie — ODER:

ABOVE: Psychological warfare and mind-shaping techniques were used during the Second World War, as in this poster dropped over Nazi-occupied Europe to create a sense of distrust in the Nazi regime. (US Army)

with assessment ratings for stability, trustworthiness, reliability, discretion, character, honesty, judgement and an unquestionable loyalty to the United States. What may not be considered are race, religion, colour, national origin, disability or proclaimed sex orientation. There are three specific and distinct categories for classification of restrained material: Confidential, Secret and Top Secret. Every CIA agent has to have the maximum security clearance for work in most sectors, although there have been cases where specific jobs call for a Secret clearance.

Access to or 'employment' by the CIA for non-US citizens is only possible for citizens in the Five Eyes countries, where a very special relationship exists for Britain, Canada, Australia and New Zealand. This is because there is a concessionary extradition restraint which allows those four countries to prosecute their own citizens in the event of a breach in national security involving the United States and not necessarily comply with extradition requests. But that works both ways. It does not apply automatically.

In one example of that, on August 27, 2019, a 19-year old British citizen was killed when the motorcycle he was riding was struck by a car driven on the wrong side of the road by Anne Sarcoolas, wife of a CIA employee working at RAF Croughton, an intelligence listening station in Northamptonshire. After fully cooperating

ABOVE: The Voice of America broadcast to the world events which helped define American ideals during the Cold War including the historic Apollo Moon missions of the 1960s and 1970s, described on radio coverage by its presenter Rhett Turner. (NASA)

ABOVE: Willis Conover broadcasting for the Voice of America in 1969, a critical time for shaping world opinion in a period of great opposition to the Vietnam War. (VOA)

with the police and providing all the information they requested, she returned to the United States and the State Department refused to fulfil an extradition order from the British government. This was on the basis that her work, and that of her husband, qualified them for diplomatic immunity.

HEARTS AND MINDS

The early days of the CIA were fraught with challenges, not least those imposed by the National Security Council which, on June 18, 1948, sanctioned covert action against the Soviet Union, forcing the agency to set up a clandestine Office of Policy Coordination (OPC). Unknown even to the director of the CIA, it answered to the Secretary of Defense, the State Department and the NSC. George Kennan, then in charge of the State Department's planning policy, was behind the OPC which gave the agency *carte blanche* to operate much like the wartime OSS and Britain's SOE, covertly disrupting the Soviet Union in its foreign policy activities. Spies came into it but destabilisation and internal chaos in Russian government activity was the aim, in which case it became the 'action' arm of the CIA in the Cold War.

In effect, the OPC was on its own, plausible deniability at the core of its operation so that there would be no direct link to the CIA, giving a free hand to agents and operatives as enshrined within its mandate and as defined through NSC 10/2: "Specifically, such operations shall include any covert activities related to: propaganda, economic warfare; preventive direct action, including sabotage, anti-sabotage, demolition and evacuation measures; subversion against hostile states, including assistance to underground resistance movements, guerrillas and refugee liberation groups, and support of indigenous anti-communist elements in threatened countries of the free world. Such

operations shall not include armed conflict by recognized military forces, espionage, counter-espionage, and cover and deception for military operations."

Within this broad band of activity and despite claims by whistle-blowers over the years, assassinations were never defined in writing, anywhere or within the implications of its mandate. But enthusiastic agents and operatives hired from the former OSS brought their unique and unusual skills to bear in carrying out a wide range of activities. Many of these men and women saw their duty as being similar to that conducted during operations against Nazi occupiers in European countries, the 'target' switched now from Nazi Germany to the Soviet Union and countries in Eastern Europe occupied by Russian forces and by the Kremlin's secret services.

During the Truman administration, the OPC prompted the establishment of the equally Top Secret Psychology Strategy Board, comprising defence and intelligence bosses who planned and executed the post-war approach to security by winning the 'hearts and minds' of people around the world. Its model grew from activities during the Korean War of 1950-1953 in which government agencies sought to proclaim a better kind of life for liberal democracies, projecting an American model of free elections and limited government controls. Intense and studious analysis of US psychological operations during World War Two were known to have created close relations with local communities around foreign bases, a great effort having been placed on winning over support for American troops in Britain to create a sense of combined purpose.

Although not directly associated with the CIA, the Psychology Strategy Board set the tone for the next 40 years during which words and phrases entrenched within the general public carried subliminal meanings to shape opinion. The Board suggested, and the US government widely implemented, the word 'containment' covering US activity

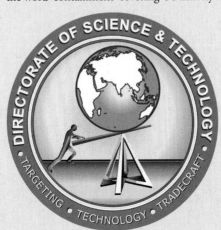

ABOVE: Founded in 1947, the CIA Directorate of Science and Technology was instrumental in developing unique devices for obtaining information, from small chips to reconnaissance aircraft. (CIA)

ABOVE: Radio Moscow broadcast its own propaganda messages to the uncommitted world, countering the global transmissions of America's Voice of America. (Soviet Postal Service)

against the Soviet Union, implying that its operations were based on a defensive, and not a belligerent, strategy. In this way it became possible to accept a wide range of covert operational activity, approved by politicians and, if leaked or disclosed to the general public, as being justified to secure the personal security of Americans and their allies.

The overt application of psychological warfare, creating a frame within which the CIA and the NSA could operate, was the radio propaganda broadcasts in foreign languages to occupied countries, initially to East European listeners. From this grew the popularity of the Voice of America (VOA) radio station which would be countered by Russia's Radio Moscow doing much the same thing in the opposite direction.

At first, Russian propaganda was crude, lambasting the Americans and their allies as capitalists enslaving people and turning them into imperialists. It struck at big business in the West, decrying the use of minority groups to enrich the wealthy and finance powerful politicians. After the death of Stalin in 1953 the tone would change, Soviet propaganda messages speaking of peace and conciliation, offering hope to uncommitted nations as better way forward. It was through the more acceptable aesthetic of gentle persuasion that the Soviet agencies proclaimed their mission, offering a better and more rewarding life for all.

Of course very little of this has to do directly with spies and spying but it established a reason for conducting overt and covert intelligence gathering, projecting to the American people this work as a limited price to pay for freedom and security. It also encouraged pro-active initiatives to change regimes and tweak the leadership in both committed and uncommitted associates of

ABOVE: The headquarters building of the CIA contains full-size models of the U-2 (right), SR-71 (left) and D-21 reconnaissance probe. (CIA)

US foreign policy. The CIA grew large in those interventions, many of which were, somewhat inappropriately, aligned with US business interests and commercial deals where local support and recruitment were vital. Key to them all, however, was the use of an intelligence-gathering service to not only support US corporate and political interest but also to significantly influence the selection of those who led certain countries around the world.

AIR AMERICA

The CIA also played a notable part in supporting native forces opposed by communist groups or guerrillas threatening the stability of democratic countries or states. An early exponent of that was the agency's activity in Laos where for more than 13 years it fought North Vietnamese forces which, despite losing to those units, moved CIA Director Richard Helms to claim that "This was a major operation for the Agency… It took manpower; it took specially qualified manpower; it was dangerous; it was difficult". It also included one of the most unusual operations carried out by the CIA, involving an air transport capability it set up and named Air America.

In August 1950, the CIA secretly bought the assets of Civil Air Transport (CAT), which had been set up by Gen Claire L Chennault, a buccaneering World War Two aviator commanding both the American 'Flying Tigers' and the Chinese Nationalist Air Force, and Whiting Willauer. CAT was flying air routes across Asia and would

continue to do so while the CIA used it to fly agents on secret intelligence operations. It was used during the Korean War to fly agents on spying assignments into China on more than 100 missions where Chennault's knowledge was of immense value.

When, in April 1953, French forces asked President Eisenhower for help with weapons and equipment to fight the communists in Laos, although reluctant to send in US Air Force personnel, he authorised a group of CAT pilots specially trained to fly Air Force C-119s under Operation Squaw, air-lifting supplies from May 6 to July 16. The French were eventually defeated at the battle of Dien Bien Phu in Vietnam just 10miles (16km) from the Laotian border but not before CAT pilots had conducted 682 air drops, flying 19,808 men, women and children out of harm's way. Simultaneously, CAT flew in agents from the Saigon Military Mission in an unsuccessful attempt to place paramilitary networks in the north of the country.

From September 1955, Air America began airlifting rice supplies into famine-blighted regions of Laos, bending the work of the CIA into assistance programmes authorised by the State Department, conducting more than 200 drops delivering 1,000tons of emergency aid. But the increasing activity of communist groups attracted increased support where Air America made regular trips to makeshift landing strips in a country without radio navigation aids and only one 25W non-directional beacon in Vientiane.

From 1959, the CIA carried Special Forces to combat the Pathet Lao guerrillas, CAT pilots getting helicopter training in Japan but the expansion of CIA helicopter operations grew, along with the introduction of small fixed-wing aircraft capable of operating into and out of very short strips. As conflict with the Pathet Lao increased, the CIA was tasked with forming a Police Aerial Reinforcement Unit (PARU) which by 1960 numbered 400 trained personnel. CIA operations throughout Southeast Asia expanded considerably but in 1961 the newly sworn-in US President John F Kennedy opposed further involvement and met with Soviet Premier Nikita Khrushchev to agree a neutrality pact. The CIA withdrew its personnel and Air America stopped flying in Laos.

The CIA maintained a watch on the country where it became apparent that the 7,000 North Vietnamese Army had not left the country as agreed and this resulted in the agency training up 20,000 local tribesmen to resist the communist aggressors. Much of the training provided by the CIA was reminiscent of the OSS during World War Two, blowing up supply dumps, ambushing trucks, mining roads and harassing the enemy. As one pilot wrote to his parents regarding news announcements that the Americans were dropping air packages, "Don't be misled that I am only carrying rice on my missions as wars aren't won by rice".

After the assassination of Kennedy in November 1963, the war began to escalate and President Johnson expanded the role of the CIA in Laos and Vietnam, Air America pilots flying rescue missions with their increasing numbers of helicopters. It was the CIA that did most of the expanded operations in Laos, however, as the American involvement was kept secret and only revealed to the public in 1969. The CIA operation had been run from Udorm, Thailand, and agency analysis of the expanding war predicted that Hanoi was more concerned with its supply routes through the Laotian border than playing a realistic part in ending the conflict. Furthermore, a CIA report dated April 1970 predicted that the communist North Vietnamese believed that Laos would fall into their hands once they had won in the south. That proved chillingly correct.

Air America continued to fly CIA operations and after the Paris peace agreement on January 27, 1973, they withdrew from Laos, the last aircraft flying to Thailand on June 3, 1974, 100 aircrew having lost their lives flying clandestine and overt missions. The airline closed up shop on June 30, 1976, ending a distinguished record of paramilitary operations while CIA agents on the ground had been able to make assessments not always coinciding with those of the armed forces. It demonstrated the interoperability of coercion and conciliation in bringing sophisticated intelligence-gathering in line with ground activity to elicit local support through aid relief and direct assistance. This was unique among spy agencies across the world.

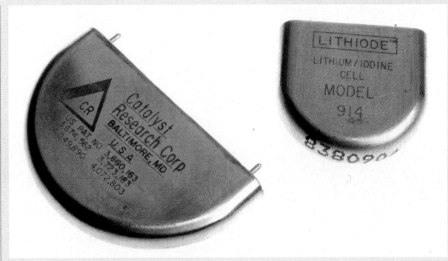

ABOVE: The lithium-iodine battery was a CIA invention that has subsequently been marketed as the lithium-ion power source for billions of separate devices worldwide. (CIA)

Since the early 1950s, the CIA had been evaluating ways to access closed countries and denied regions as a means of improving intelligence about activities threatening the future security of the United States. This involved the development of cameras, reconnaissance equipment and aircraft to conduct espionage activities where field agents were unable to reach. In the late 1950s, under Operation Tiger the CIA attempted to drop secret agents into North Vietnam but that failed to achieve the desired results and produced casualties.

Most notable in the early days was development of the Lockheed U-2 spy plane which was designed to fly at extreme altitude carrying cameras and other sensitive reconnaissance equipment during overflights of the Soviet Union. It began operating in 1956 with the expectation that it would last only a year or two before the Russians began to shoot it down. With that in mind, and while the U-2 was still in development, in cooperation with the Air Force the CIA started a spy satellite programme under the code name CORONA. The U-2 continued operating for four years until one was shot down on May 1, 1960, the year when, after several failures, the CORONA satellite achieved its first success and the aerial overflights across Russia ended.

ABOVE: A reconstruction of the Berlin tunnel created by the CIA and MI6, tapping into communication lines in the Soviet sector, a project supported by the Directorate of Science and Technology. (CIA)

The U-2 became the mainstay of aerial spy operations for several decades over areas from Central America to China and Southeast Asia while the CORONA satellites resulted in an increasingly capable and highly effective space-based reconnaissance and surveillance system. In late 1957 the CIA approached Lockheed seeking the design of a high-speed, high-altitude reconnaissance system which would succeed the subsonic U-2 and provide a much bigger platform for cameras, infrared sensors and signals intelligence equipment. Named Archangel, work on this began the following year with the initial design designated A-10 until a modified profile and appropriate materials gave it a dramatically reduced cross-section, or 'stealth', capability designated A-12 OXCART.

The A-12 took to the air on April 25, 1962, from Groom Lake, Nevada, and subsequently the CIA acquired considerable information from numerous overflights of Vietnam and North Korea before the type was retired in 1968. The A-12 was succeeded by the Air Force's SR-71, its original designation B-71 being the last in the bomber category before the numbering system started again with the B-1, a type which is still in service. The B-71 followed the XB-70 Valkyrie in the development cycle but a reconnaissance version of the B-71 bomber switched the designation to RS-71 (Reconnaissance Strategic 71), misquoted and forever known as the SR-71. The A-12 flew covert missions for the CIA while the SR-71 flew overt missions for the Air Force.

EAVESDROPPING

Throughout the Vietnam War the CIA was at variance with the US military in determining the potential outcome and defining what was really going on in the government of South Vietnam in its struggles against the communist North. The agency had concerns that the American political leadership was hearing only what it wanted to listen to and was perhaps deceiving itself as to the potential for a positive end to the conflict. As one CIA analyst reported, it believed that America was "becoming progressively divorced from reality (and that it was) proceeding with far more courage than wisdom". But the general public listened to their political leaders and failed to hear warnings from an agency whose innermost conclusions were inaccessible to the average voter.

Opposition to the Vietnam War roused tensions between protesters and civil order to such an extent that President Johnson asked the CIA to conduct a covert surveillance on US citizens in a programme known as Operation Chaos. That began in 1967 and would continue until 1974. There was some concern at Langley about this and a lot of discussion ensued as to the lines of demarcation between spying on foreign countries and eavesdropping on the American public but the justification centred on the potential connections with Soviet and Chinese communist organisations. The databank eventually carried the names and identities of more than 300,000 Americans together with organisations and sympathetic groups.

The CIA conducted Operation Chaos through police departments across the United States and by inserting secret agents into protest groups and radical political movements to gain information about their activities. This increased considerably as the anti-Vietnam War groups sought to globalise their campaign for a ceasefire and connections with other activists in Europe and the UK, concerns over rallies and marches in Britain attracting the attention of MI5 working in concert with the CIA. Considerable exchange of information took advantage of the Five Eyes agreement, in which there was a direct connection via data links between the two agencies making use of the TAT cables across the North Atlantic.

The CIA Director Richard Helms set up a Special Operations Group schooling agents in the way of the political Left-wing, anti-war supporters, having them grow their hair long and learning how to relate to such views and what to use as appropriate 'tribe-language' as the agency referred to it. Only 11 agents were deployed but they infiltrated various peace groups in the US, Europe and the UK. This operation was not directly monitored by GCHQ in England but the signals unit was made aware that CIA officers were operating in Britain so that names obtained through monitoring communications could be removed from potential police action, leaving them free to operate with impunity.

During the period up to the end of the Vietnam War and the resignation of President Richard Nixon on August 8,

BELOW: The CIA model of the Abbottabad compound where Osama bin Laden was located and which was used in a brief to President Obama for approval of a raid. (CIA)

ABOVE: Camp David, September 29, 2001, where President George W Bush (top) and National Security Adviser Condoleezza Rice and Chief of Staff Andy Card receive a briefing from CIA Director George Tenet (right). (White House)

1974, the CIA was expected to conduct a wide range of activities outside the standard conventions of intelligence organisations. Some of that involved proactively influencing national leadership in countries posing a destabilising influence on the geopolitical scene. These activities brought dissent from some agents and Congressional hearings raised by US politicians opposed to underhand methods and illegal practices. All of which was effectively a product of the CIA emerging from wartime activities and by recruiting from personnel who had conducted clandestine operations in Nazi occupied Europe.

The very essence of how the CIA conducted operations was laid bare through the Rockefeller Commission set up by President Gerald Ford in 1975 to investigate whether the agency had been involved in the Watergate burglaries. It was already known that Nixon had used intelligence agencies to further his own political standing and to use them to gain political advantage over the Democratic Party in opposition. His successor sought to clean out bad practice and the abuse of position and privilege by investigating questionable operations which also, ironically, included disclosing Project MKUltra which was a mind control programme.

Using German scientists who had been working for the Nazis on truth drugs and a wide range of psychoactive substances to induce hallucinogenic and mind-changing conditions, the CIA's Office of Scientific

ABOVE: Briefed on Russia's geopolitical activities by the CIA and the NSA, US Secretary of Defense Robert Gates (left) shakes hands with his opposite number, Sergey Ivanov, during a meeting in 2007. (Cherie A Thurlby)

Intelligence developed more advanced derivatives and experimented with them in the hope of improving interrogation techniques. It was stimulated by reports that captured Americans in North Korea and in Russia were subject to highly advanced techniques of this kind by the NKVD, then the KGB and tested by Chinese-backed North Korean scientists.

Project MKULtra was conducted in collaboration with the US Army Biological Warfare Laboratories but this was shut down shortly before the Commission released its report. Chinese and Russian psychoactive substances, biological weapons and chemical agents for use in warfare had been known for some time. This attracted the interest of the CIA in tracking these developments for antidotes and what it called 'redirectional products' capable of reversing the effects of these substances. This work would continue in cooperation with the UK defence chemical experimental establishment at Porton Down which had built an international reputation for its work on organophosphorous nerve agents initially developed in Germany during World War Two.

ABOVE: The attacks on the Twin Towers and the Pentagon on September 11, 2001, transformed the geopolitical landscape and remodelled the operating priorities of US intelligence agencies. (Andrea Booher/FEMA)

NEW SPIES FOR A NEW CENTURY

Established as long ago as 1947, the CIA is not the only US intelligence agency and in 1952 it was joined by the National Security Agency and the National Reconnaissance Office (NRO), followed by the Defense Intelligence Agency in 1961. Since then, the Department of Energy got its own Office of Intelligence and Counter intelligence (OICI) in 1977, followed by the Marine Corps Intelligence (MCI) unit the following year and the National Geospatial Agency (NGA) in 1996.

Affecting all these agencies to a lesser or greater degree, was the tragic events of September 11, 2001, when almost 3,000 people were killed in attacks on the Twin Towers, the Pentagon and in an airliner whose intended target was foiled by 40 brave passengers and crew overwhelming four terrorists, bringing it down short of its

intended target, the Capitol in Washington DC. On this fateful day, the world changed for ever, the acts of terrorism triggering a radical transformation in the way national intelligence is gathered, collated and analysed and how security agencies fulfil their mandate and carry out their responsibilities. Over the following years they saw new wars and conflict on several continents, all as a direct result of 9/11.

While there had been organisational and operational changes at the CIA over many years, the attacks of September 11, 2001, brought about the most significant transformation in its history, an evolution which would cascade through every other intelligence and national security agency. In the United States, President George W Bush expressed the desire of millions of people wanting to know why the most sophisticated

and technologically advanced intelligence agencies in the world had been unable to prevent the multiple terrorist attacks on 9/11. He also requested a full overview of the intelligence structure and sought answers to preliminary concerns that there had been too much fragmentation of sources reporting to different agencies, each with its own interpretation and very little joined-up analysis.

Completed in September 2004, the review began moving through Congress where several amendments and changes were proposed and debated, many being adopted before it was signed into law on December 17. In several ways, the ponderously titled Intelligence Reform and Terrorism Prevention Act consists of 235 pages transforming the way US agencies are structured and carry out their business. Arguably most important was the establishment of a Director of National

Intelligence (DNI) to serve as the head of the total US intelligence community, a single funnel through which all agencies would report. This individual would set the aims and objectives of US intelligence-gathering goals, structure policy so as to meet changing priorities and threats and set up a National Intelligence Program to coordinate the many separate intelligence offices. In 2012, President Obama elevated the position to cabinet level, implying that intelligence gathering was a matter for consultation and discussion at the highest level of government affairs.

Under the preceding structure, the Director of Central Intelligence was also the director of the CIA. Gone now were the days when agencies such as the CIA were left to look after the security of the nation under their own recognizance, to operate under a dark cloak opaque to scrutiny or accountability. Previously, powerful

government leaders had used the agencies for their own purposes and sometimes for commercial benefit in deals with companies in foreign countries. There had been public disquiet over the use of illegal practices and while acknowledging that these were carried out in the interests of national security, reasoned voices claimed that malpractice and rogue behaviour were counter-productive on the world stage.

The Act also required a single body to be responsible for security clearances and to have that flexible and 'mobile' so that its determinations about a person in one agency could be transferred to another if that employee successfully applied to move employment to a different intelligence agency. This allowed the transfer of a security file along with the individual concerned rather than having a separate agency look at its own criteria for clearing that same individual when he or she moved.

ABOVE: Instigator of the 9/11 attacks, Osama bin Laden sought to unite all Muslims into a single state, or caliphate. (Hamid Mir)

ABOVE: The attack on the Pentagon created a shift in protocols surrounding security clearances and on access to military facilities and institutions around the world. (US Navy)

ABOVE: John Negroponte was the first Director of National Intelligence, a post created in 2004 as a response to the decision to oversee a national intelligence programme after 9/11. (US Department of State)

In another section, the Act also established security procedures at all airports, with the Department of Homeland Security responsible for biometric screening and the creation of 'no-fly' and watch lists for individuals believed to be threats to national security. Homeland Security was also responsible for clearing all passengers on cruise ships, passing on to operators any individual who would not normally be allowed into the United States. Checking of American citizens by the intelligence community was declared as an open admission of responsibility, a line having been crossed by the shock of 9/11 which showed that the majority of Americans were in support of these stricter measures.

The precise articles of the Act kept open the possibility of stopping terrorists before they could conduct active attacks and that allowed the CIA to go after terrorist leaders known to have planned and organised previous attacks. On May 1, 2011, President Obama announced that a mixed force involving special CIA operatives and the US Naval Special Warfare Development had conducted a raid in which the Al-Qaeda leader Osama bin Laden had been killed. Old practices die hard but over the next several years a range of practices and procedures were closed, changed or modified, although the pursuit of terrorists and the leaders of organisations that have conducted terrorist acts against the United States remains.

In the last five to ten years the CIA has increasingly relied on social media to gather information about intelligence issues and threats, adopting encryption techniques that allow data to be compiled on persons of interest and on suspects in terror attacks as well as those threatening civil violence against the state. The CIA works closely at times with local law enforcement agencies or the FBI to gather together information that it believes may relate to threats at a State rather than a Federal level. These transformative changes were also increasingly reflected in the way the intelligence agencies gathered information about political adversaries in foreign countries.

Use of digital tracking and the ability to listen-in to cell-phones used by the general public, as well as by groups planning threats to national security, provided experience in applying those techniques to foreign intelligence gathering. It was no longer quite as necessary to have agents operating in the country of interest. Rather, to access communication channels and digital data highways used to connect a government's departments and offices through hacking or through the use of the Dark Web. Also, to infiltrate groups in other countries by posing as sympathetic supporters which attract conversation likely to contain classified information.

Technologies developed for use in the CIA were applied widely in the civilian sector through the same commercial companies which the US government increasingly relied upon to cut the costs of expensive, in-house development programmes. Communication companies provided technology for the domestic consumer market and these same services were leased by the government and turned to the specific needs of a particular intelligence agency. These leasing practices had been tested in the defence industry and in the US space programme for a new century in which most of the technical capabilities came from the commercial sector, rather than government research and development facilities as they had during the Cold War.

EVER INCREASING CYCLES

Over the last 25 years the role, function and responsibilities of the defence and intelligence communities has changed significantly. Threats now come directly from terrorists and rogue states which declare a riotous disruption in the affairs of democracies and liberal, elected governments. Today, there is a cycle of closed-loop intelligence nodes which when used for a single operational requirement ensure better feedback and improved results.

The cycle starts with a definition of the separate and sequential nodes. First, defined by a specific requirement, is the collection of information in an ad hoc and arbitrary fashion without a particular set of expectations. Problem solving usually starts with a defined set of requirements driving the needs which are then set out so that a solution can be found. Collecting information must not be subjective, in that if a particular set of expectations are set out, the result will be what the observer wishes to see. It cannot be that way with gathering information for intelligence purposes because the collector will not know what to specifically search for.

This is the difference between intelligence and surveillance: intelligence must be set up so as to reveal things the observer did not know was there; surveillance looks for a specific set of parameters to measure change within narrow constraints, observing them over time (temporal) with, say, a field battery, in a given location (spatial). Balancing temporal with spatial parameters sets out a chronological sequence of change which leads an analyst to conclusions about the activities and the intentions of the observed unit.

Second, after collection comes the processing of that intelligence information for utilization. That can involve translating foreign languages in text, deciphering script or decoding covert messages. Filtering is an essential part of processing and it is here that the operating protocols of surveillance kick in. Defined barriers shaped by the processing of information thus collected, reveals to the skilled

ABOVE: Newly formed directly out of the 9/11 attacks, the Department of Homeland Security is responsible for border security, including checking the authenticity of travel documents. (DHS)

ABOVE: The headquarters of the Department for Homeland Security is now at St Elizabeth's West Campus, Anacostia, South West Washington. (US Customs and Birder Protection)

The Intelligence Process

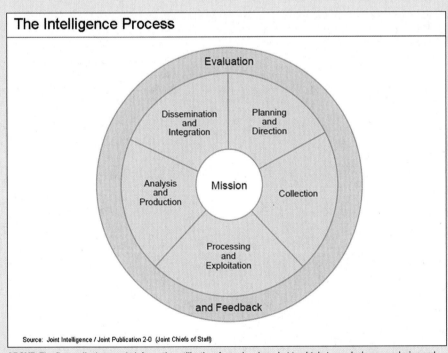

Source: Joint Intelligence / Joint Publication 2-0 (Joint Chiefs of Staff)

ABOVE: The five cyclical stages in information utilization, from planning what to obtain to producing a conclusion and disseminating the result. (DoD)

to undertake and the need to maintain a potential connection between two seemingly separate wheels to significantly improve the quality of both is incredibly hard to integrate.

It is here that comparative analysis of raw information across several separate fields of analysis is incredibly difficult to detect and in mathematical terms the probability of finding a link is inversely proportional to the number of wheels compared. For instance, a telephone conversation between a civil servant in the Russian Embassy in Paris and a colleague in an arms factory in Belarus may have nothing of interest for the intelligence analyst. Nor might a request from a field battery in the Ukraine to the Ministry of Defence in Germany for more 155-mm artillery shells seem to be relevant to the other message. But they could be connected, and it might be in this way.

The Russia-Belarus conversation could be related to the call for more ammunition in the Ukraine-Germany request in that Moscow may want to know the reaction of the French government to expanded weapons supplies from a fellow NATO member by listening to an informal conversation between the German and his colleague in Paris. But the two monitoring loops are in separate wheel cycles. How to know whether one has a specific relationship to the other, or whether the two are connected in a single strand?

observer the direction in which to prepare the data, when it is then passed to the third node in the cycle: analysis of the raw content.

Analysis takes many forms and different applications depending upon the type of information collected and processed. It can

be a closed sub-node if it provides a specific piece of data which is complete in itself. But if it locks in to other cycles it can bridge two separate closed-loop wheels that compound each, or it can provide an improved or more illuminated analysis of both wheels. Clearly, closed-loop intelligence cycles are complex

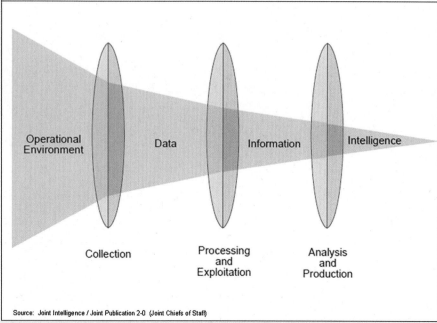

Relationship of Data, Information and Intelligence

Operational Environment — Data — Information — Intelligence

Collection — Processing and Exploitation — Analysis and Production

Source: Joint Intelligence / Joint Publication 2-0 (Joint Chiefs of Staff)

ABOVE: The integration of a thematic flow of intelligence to the completion of an analysis is achieved through a sequential narrowing of filtered flow-restrictors shaping the final and most useable elements. (DoD)

During the Cold War, that would have required intense referencing between card-file indexes with a civil servant collating and cataloguing potential links over several days if not weeks. It would have mirrored the same process as that developed at Bletchley Park and adopted by Special Branch after the Second World War. Today, those links are made by digital interconnects and by the use of highly sophisticated processing data-banks, a lot of which is covered by work at GCHQ in England or at the NSA in America.

It is within the field of analysis that the wheel moves around to the fourth node: the dissemination of the results at varying degrees of haste depending upon the urgency, timeliness or magnitude of the report. This can occupy a wide range of extreme examples. Information brought before the President each day is a report which informs that office of a wide range of national and international priorities, or it can focus on specific, time-urgent situations. Such as, for example, progress on hunting down terrorists after a major attack. Other destinations for these analyses could be related to suspected military activity by a belligerent power, or it could involve espionage activities by foreign agents. In all cases, the dissemination of reports lead to the fifth node: feedback.

To close the cycle, the feedback node ensures that results from this loop provides a firm basis for beginning the next cycle, starting again with the acquisition of raw intelligence information. Only in this case it might be more threat-specific because it will not start from the clean slate if it inherits specific strands of information. In this case it spins out to a particular set of requirements based on those results and analyses but the cycle of the five nodes continues. If nothing

has been discovered to set up a new wheel, the process begins again on another source of raw data.

In the modern world of spies and spy-agencies, complex mathematical formula, algorithms and probability analyses have taken the place of card index files and head scratching over optional investigative paths and SIGINT is the key to data-trawling and message capture. Nevertheless, the human eye and an intuitive approach to rational and irrational interpretations of received information is the key to success in uncovering the innermost workings of governments, counter-intelligence units and secret agencies manipulating information to undermine state security.

PROTECTING DEFENCE

The role played by the US Army, the Navy and the Air Force in the early years of the Cold War demanded clear and unambiguous

ABOVE: The seal of the Defense Intelligence Agency, established in 1961 to serve the requirements of the armed services at Joint Chiefs level. (DIA)

intelligence, allowing the armed services to configure their plans according to threats from Soviet ambitions. As a legacy of intelligence-gathering activities during World War Two, each service obtained its own information relevant to its role. This frequently led to conflicting interpretations and was prone to different judgements, each service 'reading' the material it obtained according to its own view of the situation.

During the post-war period the different services failed to coordinate their separate approaches to intelligence-gathering activities, frequently duplicating efforts which compromised the reliability of conclusions reached by individual armed forces. Some attempts to improve the situation were made during the 1958 Defense Reorganization Act which sought to integrate the separate services into homogenised war plans, expanding the responsibilities of the Joint Chiefs of Staff and consolidating the separate defence intelligence services.

That didn't work out as expected, coordination was non-existent and inter-service bickering prevented decisions about priorities. In the last year of his tenure as President, in 1960 Eisenhower set up a group to study seeking alternative solutions and on October 1, 1961, under the Kennedy administration the Defense Intelligence Agency began operations. Initially, it reported to the Secretary of Defense through the Joint Chiefs with the objective to cut inefficient duplication of effort and to collect, collate and distribute military intelligence through the JCS to the armed services. In reality it was to prevent the separate services from fighting for their own individual priorities and to work closer as an integrated defence force, which had been the aim of the Eisenhower administration based on the experience of the President during the Second World War.

Less than a year after it stood up, the DIA faced its first serious challenge with the Cuban Missile Crisis of October 1962. The organisation was in the midst of a phased transfer of intelligence from the separate services but that crisis demonstrated the need for combined intelligence assets and showed the separate services that a coordinated set of information improved efficiency and demonstrated that all elements of land, sea and air forces worked to the same set of data. Shortly thereafter, the DIA set up the Defense Intelligence School which helped inform the services through graduating officers returning to better integrate information and the requirements of the agency.

Throughout the 1970s the DIA bought respect and admiration through quality of information and for providing each service with specific force-related intelligence acquired by all the traditional modes of gathering data. Covering areas of US military interest, the agency supported

ABOVE: Not all employees are loyal. Ana Montes was convicted of spying while working for the Defense Intelligence Agency and given a 25-year prison sentence. (Japan Times)

been the targets of double-agents, illegals and infiltrators. With more than 15,000 employees, the majority of whom are civilian, the DIA has experienced radical change in its mission priorities and 9/11 was a seminal moment in utilising global resources through the more than 140 overseas stations in many countries. Requirements change with the geopolitical situation and today its reports on the major expansion of China's military capability have replaced those from the Cold War on Soviet-era threats.

Working for the DIA has stiffer requirements than for other US intelligence organisations, including the National Security Agency – failure of a single polygraph test excludes employment – and frequent tests are required to keep the agency current with its staff. Over time, the DIA has employed foreign nationals to work as its agents and despite security measures, the agency has not been immune from some employees acting as double agents, selling secrets to enemy states or to those with competing interests. Cooperation with friendly countries allows DIA personnel to obtain information about foreign terrorist groups and the agency has frequently helped prevent attacks on allied states through sharing access to incriminating data.

Some people within the international intelligence community believe the DIA to have a tougher interrogation policy than the CIA on 'persons of interest'. It demands stronger commitments from employees, allowing no margin for incompetence or error. Primarily committed to providing the armed services with military intelligence, the DIA is also strongly connected to the geopolitical interests of the United States, the recipient of criticism from several sources

ABOVE: The commemorative plaque on the wall of the Defense Intelligence Agency headquarters remembers those who lost their lives in service and who can be named. (DIA)

operations in the Middle East, Chile, Sri Lanka and the fallout from the Vietnam War where prisoner exchanges helped identify areas of continuing military interest, including the rise of China as a major player in Southeast Asia. But it was in the publication of the annual *Soviet Military Power* beginning in 1981 that Defense Secretary Caspar Weinberger informed the services generally, and the civilian population at large, about the magnitude of the threat from the Russian state.

Over time the DIA grew in size and influence and some have mistakenly compared it to Russia's GRU (Military Intelligence) but the two are completely different, although it is true that each has operated human spies and both have

including those campaigning for a more nuanced approach to the use of force in the interests of national security.

Because of its uncompromising and tough image, the DIA has frequently been represented in fictional depictions through TV programmes such as *The Brave*, and in a wide range of major motion picture films including *The Equalizer* series and the now famous *The Men Who Stare at Goats*. Nevertheless, admired or loathed, the US Defense Intelligence Agency continues to figure large in the story of US military and geopolitical capabilities.

ABOVE: USNA *Observation Island* conducts electronic sweeps for the DIA to maintain surveillance on compliance by foreign parties with ratified arms control treaties. (US Navy)

There are spies and counter spies, agents and double agents – and then there are 'illegals', people embedded in civil communities to manoeuvre themselves into key positions where they report activities to a foreign power. The word refers specifically to a programme of Russian agents set up after the Cold War and operated in various forms ever since, primarily in the United States but also, to a lesser degree, in the UK.

With the collapse of the communist state in 1991, one element of the KGB was re-set as the SVR, the Russian Federation's foreign intelligence service, along with the Federal Security Service (FSB) which prioritised on civilian and domestic affairs, and military intelligence, or GRU. Those organisations rebuilt the intelligence gathering, espionage and subversive practices of the old KGB and GRU, even adopting some activities conducted by the NKVD to extract information from captured agents and to eliminate those likely to be offensive to the regime.

ABOVE: In 1993 Yeltsin attacked the Russian Supreme Council building, dissolving the Russian parliament and declaring himself President, factors which rang alarm bells among Western intelligence sectors. (Bergmann)

RESIDENT ROGUES

When Yeltsin overthrew the reformed communist state under Mikhail Gorbachev, he unleashed domestic government institutions and agencies to exploitation by emerging power barons, turning a blind eye to the practices of the oligarchs constrained by his predecessor. To protect the financial interests of billionaires who achieved their wealth on the back of 'privatised' state departments previously run out of Moscow since the 1920s, the re-energised security services operated outside the law and with malice against those standing in the way of profit and wealth.

Remarkably quickly, the Russian Federation sought parity with the West as its power base shrank. During the last days of the Cold War, Russia boasted 9% of the world's population and 10.4% of its economy, shrinking to 2.3% and 2.5%, respectively by the 2020s. Immediately after the collapse of communism and shrinkage of the state, the national intelligence services recognised that they needed leverage over Western countries to maintain credible technologies and a technically robust defence infrastructure. Espionage and data-mining of high-powered Western companies grew exponentially, fuelling research into hacking governments and companies to better understand what they were developing and acquire competitive technologies.

Due to falling financial rates, Russia's global share of GDP fell from 6% at the end of the Cold War to a mere 1.7% today.

By 2021, the United States had 25% of the world's GDP and even the UK had 3%. Moreover, with the population of the Federation shrinking from 483million in 1990 to 197million today, the economic base from which to draw production and growth is only 40% what it was under Premier Gorbachev. That means the state needs to do much more to maintain its position and considerably more to equal the wealth of the Western alliance, with its population of 890million. For these reasons, the FSB and associated intelligence-gathering operatives adopted completely new ways of getting information while retaining the more traditional means.

Denied the full resources of the former Soviet Union, across the United States, Russian illegals were inserted into everyday life carrying with them their fabricated lives, couples paired off in Moscow and with a complex plan to establish a life in America. From that, with forged documents including ostensibly credible birth certificates from US States, the allegedly married couple embedded themselves into suburban life and went to colleges and universities to achieve new levels of academic achievement, only this time it was real and that placed them in higher plausibility levels.

The idea was not necessarily for each to secure jobs where they would gain access to classified information, but rather to enter social circles where they could engage in informal chat and, in that way,

gain important information. To do that it became important that they were accepted as normal and ordinary people, pleasant to engage with and fully integrated within local communities, even to the point where they played sports and joined fitness centres together with friends. In addition to the illegals, American spies working for the Russians were still active and undetected, which created a crossfire interaction for the US security services.

During the 1990s the US government was keen to conduct friendship activities

ABOVE: Mikhail Gorbachev opened the possibilities of a reformed Soviet Union with liberal laws and a strong commercial orientation for a transformed communist state. (White House)

ABOVE: Here with President George H W and Barbara Bush in front of the White House, Boris Yeltsin promised much that he would later find impossible to achieve, including a capitalist element to a democratically-run Russia. (NARA)

with Russia, including proposals to sell commercial aircraft engines to Moscow, opening the American space programme to participation in the space station and expanding trade in electronic products and computers. At US government level this created an environment of cooperation, deflecting suspicion and opening new opportunities for illegals to enter the United States and normalise what would have been unimaginable commercial practices during the Cold War. The desire for trust and shared benefits from the 'peace-dividend' provided an environment in which Russian spies were relegated to novels and films. At least in the public mind.

Conciliation was a veneer and when Vladimir Putin became President in March 2000, tension increased to the level where mutual accusations of espionage activity became commonplace, briefly relaxed when the two countries worked together to bring Osama bin Laden to justice after the 9/11 terror attack on the United States in 2001. It was a short respite. Putin promoted ex-KGB officer and close friend Sergey Ivanov and FSB Director Nikolay Patrushev and replaced regional representatives with former

security officials. In February 2001 the FBI caught Robert Hanssen and a month later the US expelled four Russian diplomats who had worked with him and 46 more were asked to leave as the country sought to clear the country of spies. The Russians responded by expelling 50 US diplomats, the greatest number on either side since President Reagan expelled 80 in 1986.

But the illegals continued to operate amid a regrouping of international espionage agreements, most notable being the result of a secret treaty on exchanging intelligence information signed between Russia and China in 1992. That agreement ensured China's cooperation when Russia trained Iraqi spies and collaborated with Saddam Hussein prior to the invasion by US and British forces in 2003. Using practices first introduced by the KGB and now conducted by the SVR, China has adopted a similar policy of placing illegals in key positions, backed up by one of the most advanced and sophisticated cyber-war campaigns of the present century. But the extensive use of spies, agents and illegals went alongside practices previously carried out by the NKVD on orders from Stalin.

ABOVE: Vladimir Putin on becoming President of the Russian Federation in 2003, a portent of dramatic change and further concerns for Western intelligence. (The Kremlin, RU)

ABOVE: While stimulating industrial growth, Putin's Russia has faced severe economic challenges with a declining share of the global market and a flagging domestic market. (The Kremlin, RU)

Under Putin, the use of the SVR to conduct assassinations in foreign countries revitalised activities from the Cold War but on a much bigger scale. In 2003, MI5 acted swiftly when it was alerted to the imminent attack on Boris Berezovsky with a binary weapon. Initially, Berezovsky had helped fund Putin's power bid but fell out with the Russian leader and became an embarrassment who it was decided would be eliminated. The following year the assassination of the Chechnyan leader Zelimkhan Yandarbiyev in Qatar was bungled by the GRU, leading to the arrest of the perpetrators.

Equally shocking was the case of Alexander Litvinenko, a Russian defector who had worked for the FSB before turning against Putin's autocratic state and fleeing the country. From his new home in Boston, Lincolnshire, England, Litvinenko wrote two books before he too was poisoned in 2006 leading to his death on November 23. In March 2018, former GRU officer turned double agent for the British and in England after he was exchanged for Russian illegals, Sergei Skripal was poisoned by Novichok nerve agent but survived. In 2024, Alexei Navalny was given a long-term prison sentence for opposing the Putin regime and died suddenly at the notorious IK-3 male hard-labour camp in Kharp on February 16, 2024.

IN PLAIN SIGHT

The illegals programme of Russian spies embedded in US communities was not

ABOVE: FBI agent Robert Hanssen fed information to the KGB from 1979 to 2001, when he was arrested and sentenced to 15 life terms without parole. He died in 2023. (FBI)

unique to the 21st century but its scale and the methods used to acquire information, move it around, exchange connections to Moscow and ensure anonymity were sophisticated. There was no spy ring as such, no pairing of illegals being aware of others, contact only being made between one individual from each pair to affect the transfer of information. The technology employed was sophisticated and the tradecraft box compromised codes, keys, computer disks and several separate false identities.

One agent carried a specially designed laptop set up to store coded intelligence information which could be transmitted (paired) by digital signal to another laptop carried by a fellow illegal passing by in the street. Pairing of one smartphone to another is routinely used by government spies and by sophisticated private investigators, allowing a paired 'phone to tap in to the signals from another. It is technology which can be bought in specialist outlets and it is through this means that commercial fraud is conducted, including stealing bank details – which is why, however convenient it might be such details should never be put on smartphones!

Illegals were not made aware of any connection between pairs other than the identity of the one individual ordered to collect information from another. The brush-pass, or transfer of information by exchanging bags, perhaps one with documents and one with money, being the most effective as the illegals pass each other going in opposite directions. The handover occurs without either party pausing in their walk and is often synchronised to occur in an underpass where there are no cameras. This method can be used to affect a blind-pass, where an exchange is made using identical bags. These can be used to transfer documents or files, or it can be used to transfer payment, usually in low denominations which are difficult to trace.

The brush-pass is not new but it has been honed to a more effective way of

ABOVE: Hanssen used this bridge at Foxstone Park, code name 'Ellis', as a dead drop site for sending information to the KGB and on to Moscow. (FBI)

discretely conducting the transfer out of sight and away from the prying eyes of counterintelligence agents, who will count the seconds between separated camera views to calculate whether either party has stopped walking to converse, indicating familiarity, or to exchange bags. On reappearing, it is

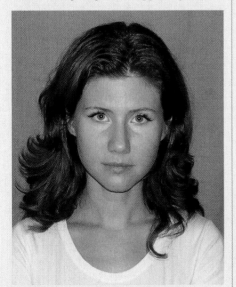

ABOVE: One of the more notorious illegals, Anna Chapman (Anna Kushchenko) got to the United States via England and, after her arrest and deportation, MI6 unsuccessfully tried to turn her to discover Russian illegals in the UK. (FBI)

impossible to tell whether there has been an exchange or not. On other occasions, illegals would meet in diners, restaurants or sidewalk cafes to openly transfer packets or files as though seeming to be two business colleagues, again an overt and open exchange deferring suspicion.

The way instructions would be transferred from one illegal to another could use disappearing ink, ad-hoc wireless transmissions known as MANETS or WANETS, or by short-wave radio transmissions. Never by smartphone pairing since that could be 'stolen' by counterintelligence agents seeking evidence of espionage. A MANET is a wireless network that does not require an existing infrastructure involving routers or 'hot-spots', each node-to-node connection being programmed as to transmitter or receptor according to the specific programmed algorithm. Usually of short range, each transmitter seeks a nearby transponder to connect to on a pre-set frequency and programme format. A WANET is a non-mobile MANET.

Use of these ad-hoc wireless networks can be from car-to-car in close proximity. Some illegals would drive from downtown residences to uptown suburbs to pass by a parked car with a receiver keyed to the MANET algorithm for connecting the two

parties and exchanging coded information. This would usually convey instructions on how to conduct 'deep-strike' data-hauling operations penetrating existing data networks, sometimes using 'geeks' to play games. These unsuspecting intermediaries connecting individuals, single members of two different cells containing illegals, would be the unwitting bridge between Russian sleepers, although that word is reserved for a completely different, albeit associated, agent.

Sleepers are completely innocuous and embedded with the same social profile of an illegal but without any active involvement in data harvesting. They are, however, involved in phishing operations where their passive role becomes active for carrying links to malicious websites, this malware being a supplementary attack tangential to a major operation bringing down a large unit such as a government department. When the primary cyberattack starts, sleepers can rise up and use malware to overwhelm security systems or compromise anti-virus software. This happened several times toward the end of the last century when China tested various programmes conducting low-level interceptions.

Another form of transferring information in coded form required no other than pieces of art or digital pictures containing coded instructions based on the frequency of the

ABOVE: The typewriter used by Chapman to transmit messages to her Russian handler via short-wave radio, possibly from a local Barnes & Noble store in New York. (FBI)

colour on the electromagnetic spectrum. Known as steganography, images observed through different filters of white, blue, green and red reveal hidden numbers with files concealed within files, an ancient form of hidden information dating to the 15th century but brought up to date through computer technology and digital image transformation. New ways of concealing information uses IP telephony to bury such hidden messages within streaming video, an excellent way of sending messages to agents over the Internet.

More conventional means of transferring information or of remunerating agents with cash, or in some cases leaving large sums of money in concealed locations, are dead-drop places where items are left for collection by another operative, sometimes years later. One illegal operating from a home address in Virginia drove far out of town to buy a shovel, moving on a few miles to dig the ground in a remote location to retrieve a stack of money which was to be used for some clandestine operation. There were instances where the mafia and organised crime gangs were used to multiply the human assets on the ground for some diversionary activity which paid them well, both to do the job and to keep silent, but such instances are very rare.

Generally, illegals are employed or receive welfare benefit, embedding them within a social services structure which hides them in plain sight. The technique of using highly visible means of income – either through wages or benefit cheques – ensures that they are enclosed within a 'sphere of credibility' which diverts suspicion about their means of support. Most illegals have good jobs, however, and make special efforts to take out bank accounts, loans, a mortgage and insurance so that they appear as completely normal, self-sufficient citizens, just like everyone else. Some transient illegals

who move frequently between jobs rent accommodation and build credit-ratings which gives them a solid base which alleviate them from suspicion.

When the illegals were set up, they demonstrated their effectiveness by providing information on a wide range of political policy positions from Latin America to Middle East countries and from how the foreign policy of Russia was interpreted to how the US military was maintaining currency with weapon systems and technology. With 1.4million personnel in uniform and perhaps a further 2.3million in ancillary manufacturers and the munitions supply chain, there were ample opportunities to work in, or garner friendships with people close to, the American arms industry. Integrating multiple strands of information provided extremely valuable information across a wide spectrum.

GOTCHA!

Through various means, not least by defecting agents from the SVR and the GRU, the FBI became aware of illegals around the year 2000 and over the next 10 years supported what turned out to be the biggest operation they had ever put together. For a variety of reasons, evidence was hard to assemble, not least because each illegal pair had operated alone and their nodes of contact were brief and difficult to observe. In some instances, FBI agents posed as a contact from another cell and obtained incriminating information by that means. But it was isolated and the FBI realised that this was far bigger than anything they had encountered before.

Information was shared with the British, who played a part through the unique facilities and capabilities for supporting back-door intercepts and when the FBI learned that the Canadians were about to make an arrest there was no time to delay.

It transpired that the Canadian authorities stayed their hand far longer than had been expected but the FBI swooped and gathered up 10 illegals who formed the core of people of interest and who had been watched for some time.

Arrested in 2010 were Anna Chapman (Anna Vasil'evna Kushchenko), Juan Lazaro (Mikhail Anatolyevich Vasenkov), Vicky Peláez, Donald Heathfield (Andrey Bezrukov), Tracey Lee Ann Foley (Yelena Vavilova), Richard and Cynthia Murphy (Vladimir and Lidiya Guryev), Michael Zottoli (Mikhail Kutsik), Patricia Mills (Nataliya Pereverzeva) and Mikhail Semenko. There were others and shortly after, Christopher Metsos (Pavel Kapustin) was taken into custody as the SVR agent who alone connected the various illegals and fed them money. Still later, Microsoft employee Alexey Karetnikov was arrested and deported.

Following court hearings, the 10 illegals were deported to Russia in exchange for British and American spies languishing in Russian prisons, among which was Sergei Skripal. There was irony in the lack of exchange between President Obama and President Medvedev over this dramatic sequence of events, for fear it would sour relations between the two countries, were there to be the usual recriminating exchanges common during the Cold War. Neither side wanted to upset the delicate balance between Russia and the Western alliance, not least because of trade deals and arms limitation talks. But that quickly turned sour when Russia began to pull away from these agreements.

On their arrival in Moscow the 10 illegals were placed under intensive interrogation in the belief that some of them may have betrayed their functions to the American authorities, been recruited as double-agents or simply been sloppy in their procedures. Several expressed a desire to recruit their

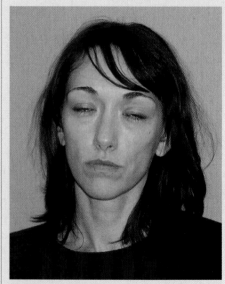

ABOVE: Patricia Mills (Natalya Pereverzeva) lived in the Seattle, Washington, area with Michael Zottoli (Mikhail Kutsik) and had been working for the Russians since 2004. (FBI)

children into the agency, after declaring that they had been prepared to do that while they were in the United States. In an interview with Larry King on CNN, Putin expressed his admiration for the illegals, saying that they had done nothing that would damage the United States and were only there to maintain a line of contact in the event that diplomatic relations between the two countries broke down.

Many illegals had come to the United States during the 1990s and spent 10-15 years living ordinary lives, only gradually increasing their clandestine activity from secured employment where they were of advantage to Moscow, and later to Beijing or perhaps more significantly to Pyongyang and the North Korean ruler Kim Jong Un. A network that has gained strength since the attack by Russia on Ukraine in February 2022 includes those three countries. Arms deals between all three have ensured that China plays soft-cop while North Korea plays bad-cop in the way each country infiltrates the West. They do that to determine political moves in the US, the UK and EU countries as they implement measures to oppose Russia – the 'hard man' in its aggression against the Ukraine.

Any definitive conclusion about the value of the illegals will await a full reflection in the future which could probably include declassified archives of material gathered by the FBI and by the NSA and the DIA as a consequence of this outstanding detective work by the US security agencies. The FBI

ABOVE: Seen here via a surveillance camera, the money-man for the illegals, Christopher Matsos (Pavel Kapustin), was arrested in Cyprus but released and exfiltrated to Russia by the SVR. (FBI)

maintains that this operation broke new ground in techniques employed to trap them and in the disclosures it brought on the way the SVR deployed highly advanced techniques. All Federal security agencies and State police forces learned new ways to detect and to hunt down illegals and their conduits to foreign countries.

Today, there are illegals operating in many countries around the world and China has proven to be a particularly active player in the game of sleeper agents working in tech

companies and throughout organisations consulting with and operating on behalf of Western countries. Coupled with the enormous advances in computer technology, remote probing, hacking activities and invasive sciences, Russia, China and North Korea operate almost with impunity in countries still uncommitted to allegiance with Western democracies, as they seal military trade deals with countries such as Iran, Syria and other players on the geopolitical edges of the free world.

ABOVE: Captured during FBI surveillance, Richard Murphy (Vladimir Guryev) and his wife Cynthia (Lidiya) operated as a married couple out of New Jersey and sought influential positions of employment for spying purposes. (FBI)

THE RUSSIA STORY

After the Cold War and from the early 1990s Russia's security, intelligence and counterintelligence services went through a thorough transformation. The Soviet-era KGB was dissolved largely because it had fought against Boris Yeltsin and his radical programme of deconstructing the communist government. Initially, the core of the KGB was reconstituted as the Ministry of Security, from 1994 rebadged as the Federal Counterintelligence Service (FSK) under the control of the Russian President. The following year it was renamed again, as the FSB but with expanded powers, penetrating domestic life in addition to conducting cooperative operations with the Foreign Intelligence Service (SVR) with personnel not so very different to those employed by the KGB.

In 1998, Vladimir Putin was placed in charge of the FSB with instructions from Yeltsin to expand its operations against the Chechen separatists through intelligence-gathering operations, followed up with an aggressive suppression of those groups. Several further reorganisations took place,

ABOVE: The coat of arms of the Soviet Union from 1956 to 1991 before it metamorphosed into the Russian Federation at the end of the Cold War. (Novosti)

its work expanded in 2003 to absorb the activities of the Border Guard Service of Russia which has a strength of more than 210,000 personnel. After a series of attacks on civilian facilities in Moscow by Chechen terrorists, further powers were granted which

allowed the FSB to take over the control of other security-related organisations, effectively ending bitter role-disputes and centralising government control onto a single body.

These amalgamations and integrated controls put sole power into the hands of the Russian President and effectively made him head of all its operations, expanding the grip on the FSB to a greater degree than Stalin had over the NKVD. In this way, Russia has become an autocracy run by a dictator and the operation of its spy and security agencies is central to the state's domestic and foreign policy programmes. This was consolidated when Putin addressed a meeting of highly placed FSB officials on June 28, 2004, when he defined the three separate roles of the organisation: counterespionage; protecting the economy and the financial health of Russia; and defeating organised criminal gangs, some of which were a legacy from the Yeltsin days of oligarchs and crime barons.

By 2008 oppressive and focused attention to terror attacks had paid off, special FSB groups such as the Spetsnaz units carrying

ABOVE: The headquarters of Russia's Foreign Intelligence Service, the SVR, located in the Yasenevo District outside Moscow city centre. (Alex Saveliev)

ABOVE: Vladimir Putin was head of the Federal Security Service from 1998-1999, raising its powers to a higher level than had been the position of the KGB during the Soviet era. (RIAN)

out assassinations and killings to drive down the number of incidents from 257 in 2005 to 48 two years later. Integrating domestic and foreign operations, the FSB were able to use agents to cut off the foreign supply of arms to terrorist groups and set the scene for interventions in other countries to shut down the supply of weapons. Some of these operations were scaled to the threat, in one incident an armed convoy being attacked killing 12 people. By 2010 most of the rebellious groups on the outer periphery of the Russian Federation had been neutralised and the FSB became convinced that hard-line tactics were essential to success.

It was not to last. Suppression of ethnic rights, anti-Semitism and Islamophobia fuelling discontent and violence against the Russian State. Bombings in Moscow's Metro system during 2010 and an increasingly hard-line approach by police and security staff gave President Medvedev the excuse to expand still further the powers of the FSB. From July 2010, the security service had authority to issue its own warnings to civilians according to how it interpreted threats, carrying a prison sentence of 15 days if ignored. It gave the agency added confidence and boosted its responsibility for using decades of experience in conducting disruptive activity in foreign countries by assuming responsibility for leading the SVR and GRU units as Russia's territorial ambitions looked to the West.

A danger with any top-heavy government organisation, the FSB had its own levels of corruption and misuse of funds and resources. Over time it came under criticism from other Russian government bodies but the successes it achieved in

securing the country supressed any serious challenges. Putin made a publicly declared policy of eliminating corruption but the interpretation of what constituted that was a judgement left to the observer and very little investigation was made. Nevertheless, Putin continued to stand before media cameras and flaunt his alleged anti-corruption credentials.

CRAFTING POLICY

In the post-Cold War restructuring, the SVR was formed in December 1991 and took prime role for foreign intelligence-gathering operations from its headquarters in the Yasenevo District of Moscow with a focus on civilian affairs, leaving the military function to the GRU. The SVR deploys agents overseas but only a small fraction of total Russian operatives work outside the country. Nevertheless, Putin rates the SVR highly as it proudly claims its origin to the establishment of the Cheka in 1920. During a visit in 2020 he met several former chiefs, operatives and foreign agents as well as spies from the UK including George Blake.

Under Russian law, the SVR has responsibility for counterintelligence, for 'active' measures which involve bugging, break-ins, assassination and setting up disruptive activities in foreign countries. It has full authority under the State to conduct military and economic espionage involving the extraction of technological secrets from other countries and joint operations with other government establishments. It has responsibility for the protection of Russian citizens overseas and for carrying out electronic surveillance in other countries. It reports directly to the Russian President and is a permanent member of the Security Council of Russia, which coordinates all activities of a military and national security nature.

The SVR has had a chequered history and increased both its power and its value during the Yeltsin years in the final decade

ABOVE: A Chechen fighter pauses for a cigarette during the war against Spetsnaz units of the FSB. (Author's collection)

of the last century, taking a proactive stance on interpreting the foreign policy objectives of Russia to the point where it disagreed with the Premier on several occasions. It politicised its own objectives and interpreted history as a prelude to post-Cold War Russian policy, aspects ignored in the West and now recognised as precursors to a more belligerent approach to national aims and objectives.

One example of that is the way the SVR openly 'educates' Russian people into the historic 'right' of the country to take back possession of the Baltic States, to reabsorb the Ukraine into the borders defined under Tsarist Russia and to move inexorably toward the reoccupation of buffer states against what it interprets as an aggressive and threatening group of West European countries. The SVR has distributed CDs and DVDs which proselytise this message and it has taken a front role in the use of overt and covert

ABOVE: Russian FSB Spetsnaz soldiers during operations against terrorists in the Northern Caucasus in 2008. (Novosti)

ABOVE: Yevgeny Primakov, first head of the SVR from 1991 to 1996 who verified that it was the KGB that fuelled the anti-gay propaganda myth that AIDS was created by the US government. (Novosti)

techniques and tradecraft to undermine Western democracies, sever US interests from those of other NATO countries and forge links with pro-Russia groups in former territories of the Soviet Union.

Active measures also include eroding Western confidence in partnerships and alliances which Russia sees as counter-productive to its own foreign policy objectives and in recent years these have increasingly involved cooperative espionage programmes with anti-American interests. The SVR was a major player in getting Russia into the Iranian nuclear weapons programme, a legacy of British support for a nuclear power initiative in the days of the Shah which stopped after the Islamic revolution overthrew the pro-Western leadership. During the 1990s, considerable assistance was provided by Russia, which supported the switch to nuclear weapons, and the SVR was fully engaged with making that happen.

The SVR also shaped the way the country viewed NATO and the Anti-Ballistic Missile Treaty and became more prominent than the Foreign Ministry, whose diplomats increasingly worked under the protocols laid down by this agency. Russia has consistently integrated civil and military affairs, in their nuclear programme where power production and weapons are served by the same organisations, and in their space programme where there is no clear and reconcilable line between the peaceful and scientific exploration of space and the development of military capabilities. Today these aspects are generally regarded as evidence of Boris Yeltsin's statement in 1999 that the SVR was the principal government organ for foreign policy, uniquely so among major powers.

For these and other activities, in May 2023, the US Treasury has placed sanctions on the SVR for its conduct in foreign affairs and because of its expansion of intelligence operations after the unveiling of the illegals by the FBI in 2010. Working with the FSB, the SVR built a successor group which had its own defectors and informants. The British security services are aware of several thousand Russian agents who have entered Western countries legally and operate under deep-cover to join political organisations, undermine democratic governments, sow disinformation, spread falsehood through social media and create a sense of dissatisfaction among ordinary voters.

ABOVE: Currently the head of the SVR, Sergey Naryshkin opened an exhibition in 2016 with the title 'Ordinary Fascism', displaying alleged war crimes by Ukrainian security forces. (Duma.gov.ru)

Informants have named agents involved in such activities and these included high-profile names such as Robert Hanssen and Aldrich Ames. Some of these people have been exchanged for Russian spies held in American jails but the majority go unknown, freely operating in countries across the Western world. In some instances, the CIA and the DIA have worked against the Russians to disrupt their information channels, to obtain the identity of contacts and the identity of FSB/SVR agents operating in the West. Such operations are rare but, where they do exist the hunting down of SVR agents is a key activity by Western intelligence operatives.

A major agreement was reached with China in 1992 in which the SVR signed a cooperative deal with Beijing's Intelligence Bureau of the Joint Staff Department. This organisation is China's principal military intelligence organisation and reports directly to the People's Liberation Army but it also has general intelligence, counterintelligence and subversive roles to play. The SVR has more recently masterminded the deal by which Russia supplies gas and oil to China to power its vast manufacturing industries and to protect those interests by carrying out surveillance on oil pipeline deliveries between West European countries.

Specifically, the attacks on the Nord Stream 1 and 2 pipelines in September 2022 were a combined control-bid and

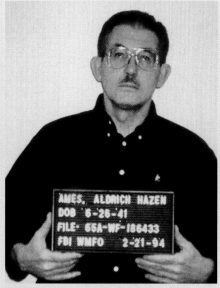

ABOVE: Convicted of spying for Russia, the CIA counterintelligence officer Aldrich Ames is currently serving a life sentence in a Federal Correctional Institution in Indiana. (FBI)

demonstration of intent should Russia wish to undermine European options. Putin had already claimed the right to interfere: "If our Western colleagues continue the obviously aggressive stance, we will take appropriate retaliatory military-technical measures and react harshly to unfriendly steps. I want to emphasize that we have every right to do so." Energy protection and

shaping foreign use of energy and power supplies is now a priority for the SVR and a wide range of operational techniques are employed to penetrate Western activity through electronic and human infiltration to distribution networks.

There is ample evidence that the SVR, with or without the help of the FSB, periodically carries out assassinations in foreign countries of defecting agents and others of embarrassment to the system. The SVR also 'hires out' its services to friendly countries for protecting their officials and government representatives. It is also active in penetrating electronic libraries and databanks used by the general public in foreign countries, planting subtle shifts in data and information to distort facts and change the tone of collated information. This is usually done to create a positive view of Russia and to discredit the United States and its Western allies.

In Russia, the SVR openly recruits agents, much in the way that MI5 in Britain and the CIA in Washington actively and openly seeks out people to work for their respective organisations, frequently advertising for applicants. But the criteria for the SVR and the FSB has changed and allegiance to the principles of Marxist-Leninism no longer haunts the interview room. Instead, love of the mother country and strict loyalty to the Russian state is an uncompromising requirement. Adherence

ABOVE: Key to bringing down Aldrich Ames were FBI mole-hunters (from left) Sandy Grimes, Paul Redmond, Jeanne Vertefeuille, Diana Worthen and Dan Payne. (FBI)

ABOVE: A Russian Kashten-class ship about to launch an AS-26 deep submergence submarine vessel of the type believed to have sabotaged the Nord Stream 2 pipeline in the Baltic Sea. (Mil.ru)

to national policy is more firmly entrenched in the Russian security services, while in Britain and the United States a wider, albeit moderate, political view is no obstacle to employment. The SVR screens applicants for appropriate jobs and responsibilities and assigns departments within the organisation according to skill and aptitude.

SETTING THE BATTLE SPACE

While the SVR had been driving the foreign policy advice to the Kremlin, largely put into play by Putin since he increased the powers of this agency, initially the FSB had a leading role in convincing the political leadership to invade Ukraine. An activity which began 20 years ago when the Orange Revolution saw Yukashenko and Yanukovych struggle for political supremacy on policies largely divided between pro-EU or pro-Russian alignment. The legacy of Soviet domination forged opposition from the people and their leaders.

Since the extensive destruction of World War Two and liberation from German occupation by Soviet forces in 1944, the Ukraine had rebuilt its industrial base as one of the primary providers of military equipment and weapons, becoming one of the most important republics answering to Moscow. After the death of Stalin in 1953, in a process of renewal and trust Khrushchev transferred the Crimea to Ukraine as a friendship gesture which divided opinion both in that country and in Russia, an

enduring irritant for Russian citizens in that peninsula.

After the collapse of the Soviet Union, political opinion in the newly independent Ukraine polarised around pro-Western versus pro-Russian affiliation and between socialism versus capitalism, with a minority of Ukrainians favouring stronger ties with Russia and a less free-wheeling economy. For much of the period after gaining independence, Russia leased naval facilities on Crimea for its Black Sea fleet but an increasingly pro-Western alignment in the Ukraine served notice that the fleet must withdraw by 2017. Following which Russia planned to relocate its naval forces to the port of Tartus on the north-west coast of Syria, allowing direct access to the Eastern Mediterranean Sea without having to negotiate the Bosporus.

But the FSB had other ideas and influential policy-shapers Nikolai Patrushev, Yuri Kovalchuk and Alexander Bortnikov, all members of Putin's inner circle with close ties to the FSB and the national security framework in the Kremlin, adjusted the agenda. Each man has a strong and powerful base and fed Putin with extreme views regarding foreign policy and future objectives. From the immediate post-Cold War period, Russia's intelligence services had penetrated Ukrainian politics and infiltrated the country's own security service, the SBU, planting agents and recruiting SBU members to work for Moscow and with some success.

Uncertain about a way forward, Putin sought to regain control over lost territory from the collapse of the Soviet Union and looked back to Russia's imperial past to restore control over vast swathes of Eastern Europe. Bortnikov was a key player in persuading Putin to take military action. But that came after a lengthy struggle that began in 2014 when FSB agents added encouragement to ambitious plans to arm separatist groups in the Donbass where Russian commando units deployed troops and arms for open confrontation in an area heavily populated with sympathisers. Before the annexation of Crimea in 2014, Ukraine's President Victor Yanukovych signed a further deal allowing the Black Sea fleet to remain in the Crimean peninsula until 2042.

The role played by the FSB placed it at the top of the intelligence services preparing the way for an invasion of Ukraine but levels of corruption, widely reported in leaked comments from former and current agency personnel, reached a level where a delusional approach to analysis favoured reports to Putin which supported his own desires. He was simply hearing what he wanted to listen to. But the FSB was itself assured of a situation far from reality and while the SBU was working to eradicate moles and informants among its own ranks, the FSB was feeding directly into the Ukraine with agents living among locals to provide a realistic picture of trends within the population *vis-à-vis* Russia and closer ties to Moscow.

BELOW: The headquarters of the FSB in Kuznetsky Most street, Moscow, from where subversive operations are planned to disrupt government activity in unfriendly countries. (Stan Lobov)

To counter this, FSB personnel moving into the Ukraine were tracked by the CIA, MI6 and other intelligence services from several European countries and they worked with Ivan Bakanov, the head of Ukraine's SBU to counter FSB infiltrations. As Russian troops gathered along the border with Russia and Belarus offered support to Moscow, the war was widely anticipated long before it began. Not least because senior Russian and former Soviet intelligence officers were observed moving to the region from places as far off as Cuba and Africa to focus on gathering information about the possibility of popular support for a Russian 'liberation'.

One of these was Sergey Beseda, a veteran KGB officer from the 1970s who had responsibilities for Ukraine, Moldova and Georgia and who since 2013 had been working to use active measures and deadly force to push for a pro-Russian government

in the Ukraine. To support that, after the Russian's moved into the Donbass in 2014, FSB agents were set up in dozens of Ukrainian cities to provide information about the susceptibility of the country to a military takeover. Activity became so intense that all the major intelligence organisations of the Western world focused on these operations.

The judgement was seriously misplaced when, supported by the CIA, the advice to the Ukrainian leadership was that Russia was bluffing and unlikely to invade, that it could not risk the response from NATO countries. The British security service disagreed and cautioned the Ukraine that Moscow was in all probability looking to install a pro-Russian leader in Kyiv, even suggesting that Yevhen Murayev, leader of a banned political party, was a potential candidate for such a coup. So concerned were the British that in January 2022 Foreign Minister Liz Truss

sent a message that it would "not tolerate Kremlin plot to install Russian leadership in Ukraine". Russia replied that it was "NATO countries led by the Anglo Saxons that are escalating tensions around Ukraine".

But the FSB agents operating in the Ukraine were living in flats and apartments from where they sent back their reports, operations being much easier due to their familiarity with public services and urban versus rural conurbations from years of experience living in the country during the Cold War. Senior FSB personnel were monitored by the SBU and in the closing weeks prior to the attack communications began to increase and signals were monitored between Russian operatives and airborne units of the Russian military, a highly unusual and worrying activity, joint operational planning now being self-evident.

Sensing things were hotting up, in mid-February 2022 Ukraine's foreign intelligence service, the SZRU, sent its own agents into Russia to spy on military units where large numbers of tanks and armoured personnel carriers were encountered in the village of Potemkin. Some encounters were bizarre. Written reports sent back by Ukrainian spies noted that some Russian units were apparently in chaos, equipment straddled across roads and highways, trucks partially abandoned due to their crews bartering fuel for alcohol. Blind drunk, Russian soldiers were reeling all over the country roads with no apparent discipline or operational priority. It was from these areas that initial reports of abusive behaviour and rape originated.

In Germany, intelligence chief Bruno Kahl noted that there had been SIGINT

ABOVE: A key and influential adviser to Putin, Nikolai Petrushev (left) was instrumental in moving Russia toward a more hostile pressure on the Ukraine. (Kremlin.ru)

ABOVE: Petrushev, Kovalchuk and Bortnikov supported militant separatists in the Donbass region of Ukraine and drew up plans for Putin's approval to provide arms and to conduct false-flag operations. (Andrew Butko)

ABOVE: Ivan Bakanov headed up the SBU, Ukraine's intelligence organisation, in pursuit of FSB agents who were already sending confidant messages to Putin that Ukrainians would welcome a Soviet 'liberation'. (Government of Ukraine)

intercepts to indicate that Putin was still undecided as to what course to follow and he was so personally sure that the Russians were playing a bluff that he was still in Kyiv when the attack came on February 24, 2022. He was not alone in that belief and the view from President Zelensky's own intelligence reports judged that Russian operations were a psychological ploy, despite cautioning that missile strikes and commando units might parachute in to the Ukrainian capital and attempt to topple the government.

FIGHTING BACK

The core deception was at the heart of FSB dysfunctionality. Granted too much power by Putin himself, the organisation had fostered corruption through a sense of self-aggrandisement and hubris, believing that as long as it verified the Russian leader's own conclusions, all would be well. FSB officers funded their own high living in the Ukraine from agency funds, feeding Putin with reassurances that the people would welcome Russian troops and stand aside while they toppled this 'fascist' government. Unsure at first, Putin was duped into accepting this view by a spy agency serving its own ends at the cost of realistic analysis.

Ironically, the Ukrainian intelligence services were a direct legacy of the KGB, its headquarters in Kyiv being in the same building as that occupied by its Soviet masters during the Cold War and operating along the same bureaucratic lines. There was concern that the staff and many agents were probably pro-Russian and that in the event of an invasion their loyalty could be called into question. In reality this was not the case and while FSB agents were discretely leaving their homes and travelling east, preparations were being made for some form of national defence from air attack and subversive activity. Ukrainians knew the tactics of Russian operatives and feared that there were secret agents and spies lurking in the shadows ready to conduct guerrilla activity.

A major concern of the Ukrainian spy agency had been the sheer size of the organisation, some 27,000 employees being on the payroll of the SBU, compared with little more than 5,000 for the UK's MI5. Through politically uncommitted members of the SBU, the FSB had attempted to

ABOVE: Busy days for employees at the SBU intelligence-service headquarters in Kyiv, Ukraine, as dark war clouds gather. (Kiyanks)

recruit double-agents and in this they had some success. Over time, these would be weeded out and put on trial while the overall majority were instinctively supportive of the Ukrainian government's stance over Russian aggression. But the FSB had been trying for several years to get back deep inside the inner workings of the SBU and they achieved the success they did largely because the structure was unchanged from its earlier days and had exploitable vulnerabilities.

Cleansing the SBU of double-agents continued for a long time into the war, Zelensky purging the organisation of traitors and replacing Bakanov due to his incompetence in cleaning up the organisation, putting Vasyl Malyuk in charge. Immediately after the war began, from America the CIA and the NSA broke Russian codes and delivered encrypted cell-phone equipment with intercept capabilities for finding fifth-columnists and other suitable targets. Large numbers of Russian sympathisers were rounded up and put on trial, the Zelensky government taking a tough stance on agents from Russia and a few from Belarus.

Following the activities of its former KGB self, the SBU continued to operate in an active role, penetrating enemy territory and infiltrating denied areas to conduct sabotage and disrupt transport and communications. SBU units have been responsible for attacking the Kerch Bridge in the Crimea and of blowing up munition dumps and other targets of interest. Some operatives

have said that they model their activities on those of the British SOE during World War Two and blend the tactics and methods of espionage and counterintelligence operations with guerrilla warfare. They operate fast-moving inshore boats and use unmanned aerial vehicles (UAVs) to deploy sensors and scanners in remote areas to monitor nocturnal enemy movements which attempt to avoid detection.

The combined activities of spying and conducting clandestine operations had an established record in the SBU, units of which had infiltrated the Donbass in 2019 to get to Vladimir Tsemakh who had controlled the air defence operations in Snizhne when a Buk 9M38 missile shot down a Malaysia Airlines Boeing 777 airliner with the loss of 298 lives. The capture of Russian personnel accused of war crimes became an objective of the SBU but activities were curtailed so that resources could be confined to the use of the security services on sabotage operations.

Continued use of more conventional spying and intelligence-gathering activity became increasingly important as signals equipment was attached to remote-controlled weapons such as UAVs and autonomous platforms which carried GPS trackers for position accuracy. Increasingly, SIGINT was a vital means of intercepting coded and encrypted messages between military units and the use of satellite communications added new tasks to existing

requirements. The intelligence services of the US, the UK and European countries lent their support to extracting useful intelligence from signals intercepted by land, sea, air and space-based assets.

Intelligence agencies provided much of the information upon which initial reactions were based, an underestimation of the ability of the Ukrainians to resist attack,

ABOVE: Ukraine's SBU agents capture a Russian agent reconnoitring prior to the Russian invasion. (Government of Ukraine)

ABOVE: US intelligence monitoring of the situation in early 2022 as Russian forces mobilised close to the border with Ukraine are displayed on this briefing chart. (US Intelligence Services)

the ineptitude and almost casual manner in which the Russian military appeared to be rolling along the paved roads of the country confounded conclusions. This accounts for the initial reluctance of the NATO partners to commit to support for Ukraine and for their supply of aid and munitions to be delayed. As the war expanded and the Russians were pressed back from their initial gains, the use of covert and overt intelligence-gathering increased.

With diversification of production from Russia's internal manufacturing industry to supplies of war-related materiel from China, North Korea and Iran, the use of espionage techniques to track supply routes increased. It drew in the full resources of the NATO countries, the European Union and the Five Eyes nations to provide Ukraine with information and analysis of benefit to it on the battlefield, in its offensive against Russian targets on land and at sea and in its use of covert means to strike deep into Russian territory and erode public support for its war.

Constantly in mind, Western intelligence organisations recognised the role FSB officers had in pushing Putin toward invasion for a wide variety of reasons, a few involving self-serving interests aimed at securing power-positions within an occupied Ukraine. Notable were key players at the FSB that sought their own baronial fiefdoms and saw the Ukraine as a place where they could secure power and wield control. They fled when the tide of fortune turned against them

and they were sought out within Russia for having engineered a catastrophe.

The FSB itself paid a heavy price when only a few weeks after the stalled invasion, Putin removed it from its role as Russia's primary spy agency and placed responsibility for that with the GRU and its new boss, Vladimir Alekeyev, which the intelligence community believes was responsible for

the chemical attack on Skripal in 2018. The news was significant, displaying a very public declaration that the total occupation of the Ukraine was a long-term objective which would never be relinquished, a fact emphasised when Gen Alexander Dvornikov was given command of the operation in May 2022. Russia's military spy agency was now in control of the war and of administering

ABOVE: The Russians struck Ukraine with land and air forces on February 24, 2022, witnessed by a stunned population outside this house on Bohatyrska Street, Kyiv. (Dsna.gov.ua)

ABOVE: Russia's Minister of Defence since 2012, Sergei Shoigu (right) meets with Vladimir Putin after the withdrawal of Russian forces to the south-eastern regions of Ukraine. (Kremlin, ru)

retribution to flagging performance from the armed forces.

But a grim fate awaited Ukrainian traitors and political leaders seeking power in the event that Russia achieved victory and who took Russian money, lots of it, to deliver up victory to Moscow which, when it failed, was a deep embarrassment to Putin. Revenge was sought and few made it back to Russia but the Ukrainian intelligence services and their international allies tracked and recaptured many of those who had promised defeat and seen their own expectations evaporate under Ukrainian resistance. Even as they were negotiating with realtor's rental terms on riverside apartments in Kyiv, the FSB agents had never fully understood the Ukrainian people.

In a poll taken in April 2021, a mere nine months before the invasion, 84% of Ukrainians declared that they would consider any further encroachment beyond the contested Donbass as an occupation, a mere 2% admitting their support for Russia. These figures were never passed along to Putin and the FSB agents, living high on the hog in downtown Kyiv, continued to feed the Kremlin lies and false information. As one agent said to another when the attack began: "Depart your flat but leave the keys." The implication being that after a short while they would be back again to savour the joys of *al fresco* sidewalk cafes and the exciting social life of the Ukrainian capital.

POSTSCRIPT

Intelligence agencies in Europe and the United States are increasingly aware of activities by the SVR and the GRU in Transnistria, a sliver of Moldova alongside Ukraine which has sought breakaway status since the collapse of the Soviet Union and which bears a chilling comparison with the Donbass, where separatists were supported by Russia and then used as a springboard for attack on Ukraine itself. The FSB has also been seen working to disrupt Moldovan attempts at joining the European Union, spreading lies about government aid denied to areas of the country where there is strong support for Russia.

The pattern is familiar and the use of the intelligence services to sow dissent, recruit pro-Russian spies and set down sleepers to conduct guerrilla operations in the event of an invasion is emblematic of a geopolitical intent. The FSB in particular has been actively conducting such operations in the Baltic States for some time and that has triggered a pro-NATO stance among their populations. But the lessons learned by Moscow in more than 30 years of post-Soviet evolution for its tripartite intelligence services are exportable to pro-Russian countries and to those supplying arms to Moscow in pursuit of its military adventures,

In a practice seen as common from China's intelligence operatives, Russia's security services are now recruiting nationals in foreign countries with politically sympathetic views to carry out disruptive activities, even to the extent of using fascists disgruntled with domestic policies. Russian agents are using citizens of Estonia to sow discontent by encouraging them to attack government offices, cars carrying officials and residences of elected officials, for money. It turns the illegals programme on its head and encourages the populace to question the ability of the elected government to keep control and maintain security.

Social media is the recruiting tool used to connect self-disaffected individuals which, in a country such as Estonia that has a high percentage of its citizens identifying as Russian, covert recruitment to carry out overt acts of disruption is a cheaper alternative to embedded people from Moscow. This form of hybrid warfare elevates the importance, and the effectiveness, of national security forces and integrates the standard practices and working rationales of spy agencies into erosion of democratic government and the general disaffection surrounding conventional electoral systems, invoking a sense of inadequacy to disquiet the population and disrupt the smooth running of nation states.

Russia's determination to pre-condition countries for military intervention began with hybrid operations against Georgia before the Russian invasion in 2008, pitting Georgians against their own government through blended synchronisation of exposed vulnerabilities. After the Russian invasion of the Ukraine in February 2022, Russian synchronised hybrid warfare started against Moldova to set the international conditions for military intervention using social media and hacking activities without direct involvement of agents or intelligence-gathering operations in the country itself.

Geopolitics plays a very large part of current operations. It works as spy agencies sow the myth that the Moldovan government is withholding financial support from regions that polls show are reluctant to support the national bid for membership of the European Union, creating a sense of betrayal by the country's own leaders. None of these lies have any basis in truth but in a social-media age of judgement by accusation, it works to recruit discontented groups in a country that shares a border with the southern part of the Ukraine.

ABOVE: An early target for Ukrainian missiles, the Russian cruiser Moskva in Sevastopol. (George Chernilevsky)

HI-TECH SPIES

Obtaining information about the activities of a foreign power can take many forms, including the use of people to spy and gather details from what they heard, what they observed and sometimes what they conclude from meetings and discussions. That is HUMINT (human intelligence), another word for conventional spying. Since the advent of the camera, images can be obtained through the use of photographic equipment to take pictures of activities seen by the informant, either directly observed or by recording on film other photographs or pages of documents. This is IMINT (imaging intelligence), which can take highly sophisticated forms and extend from hand-held or remote-control cameras to aerial equipment in visible or non-visible parts of the spectrum and satellites collecting that information from space.

A third form of intelligence comes through radio communication between individuals overheard or recorded through direct access to landline connections or by harvesting digital signals conveyed through cell-phone towers to smartphones, to direct communication between antennas linking government buildings or to data transmitted through connections linking transmitters to remote receivers. This is known as SIGINT (signals intelligence). Such signals can be carrying a wide range of information in coded or open form but they allow access to perhaps even secure links through technology which in recent years has become widely available for hackers and data-harvesting activity engaged in criminal activity.

SIGINT formed the basis for accessing information during World War Two, where coded messages sent by radio signal connected military units, with command centres and established connections between separate government departments located in different places. This was the basis for the Ultra signals intercepted by radio receivers and sent to centres such as Bletchley Park in England for decoding into legible messages. Before and during the war, Germany used Enigma machines originally developed for sending confidential information between banks and financial institutions, where personal and private information could remain secure.

There is a fourth form of obtaining information which is more directly associated with battlefield operations and warfare in general, the gathering of information from electronic sensors such as radars on the ground, in the air or at sea. Passive and active defence relies on an up-to-date map of such equipment operated by the enemy and an accurate analysis of specific electromagnetic frequencies for detecting intruders or for targeting of weapons. This is electronic intelligence gathering, or ELINT, and is frequently defined as a subset of SIGINT.

Obtaining direct battlefield information saw the first use of a very overt intelligence operation when Thaddeus S Lowe introduced the concept of airborne reconnaissance by ascending in a balloon on June 18, 1861 and looking down across Washington DC, telegraphing a message to President Lincoln by a cable, recorded historically as the first message conveyed from the air to the ground in America. The feat had been encouraged by Joseph Henry, the first Secretary of the Smithsonian Institution and it proved its point. That day, Lowe's message was simple: "The city, with all its girdle of encampments, presents a superb scene." But the implication was self-evident.

Aerial photography came into its own during World War One when reconnaissance and mapping from the air became the first operational military function for the aeroplane. Cameras specifically designed for use from the air followed quickly and were brought to a new capability during World War Two where the Fairchild K-19 and K-21 were the workhorse cameras of that time. The Trimetrogon K-17 mapping camera was introduced toward the end of the war which consisted of three cameras taking one vertical and two oblique images simultaneously. The requirement for surveillance and reconnaissance during the early phases of the Cold War led to further development and resolutions of 20-25ft (7-8m) on a side at an altitude of 33,000ft (10,000m).

BELOW: Integrated with US signals intelligence operations, RAF Menwith Hill in England is instrumental in maintaining a global network managed by British and American governments and shared with the Five Eyes partners Australia, Canada and New Zealand. (Matt Crypto)

When Lockheed began work on the U-2 in 1954 the need for a camera capable of providing a resolution of 10ft (3m) at altitudes in excess of 68,000ft (20,725m) required a four-fold improvement in performance. The initial success with high-acuity cameras had been made by James G Baker of Harvard and Richard S Perkin of the Perkin-Elmer Company when they produced a 48in (122cm) focal-length scanning camera for the Army Air Force. This was tested in a B-36 over Fort Worth, Texas, which produced photographs from an altitude of 34,000ft (10,360m) in which two objects 3in (7.6cm) in size could be differentiated. But the camera weighed a tonne and was totally impractical for a tiny spy-plane so in 1954 Baker adopted an Air Force K-38, 24in (61cm) aerial framing camera which was built by the Hycon company of Pasadena, California for the U-2.

Rebadged as the A-1, it consisted of two K-38 training cameras, one fixed in the vertical and the second on a rocking mount taking alternate left and right oblique shots. The U-2 also carried a Perkin-Elmer tracking camera together with a K-17 as back-up

ABOVE: Here seen with fictitious NASA markings, the U-2 spy-plane was used by the CIA for overflights of Soviet territory and then across Cuba, China and other places in Southeast Asia. (NARA)

to the new A-1. While developing that camera, Baker began work on optical systems synthesised by computers with software algorithms, modelling lens curvature, glass compounds and lens spacing to accommodate different rays of light. This technology was used to develop the A-2 consisting of three K-38 cameras with 9.5in (24.1cm) film magazines. These were the first relatively large photographic objective lenses with several aspheric surfaces and were able to resolve 60 lines per millimetre, a 240% improvement.

This work led to the B camera, a completely new concept with a much longer, 36in (91.4cm) aspheric lens which could obtain pictures from one horizon to the other, thereby reducing weight by eliminating two lenses and shutter assemblies than the standard Trimetrogon configuration. It had an 18in x 18in (45.7 x 45.7cm) format achieved by focusing the image on two counter-rotating but overlapping 9.5in (24.1cm) wide strips of film. Early U-2 flights used the A-series camera while the B camera

15 OCT 1962

MILITARY ENCAMPMENT (MISSILE)
LOS PALACIOS, CUBA
22-40N 83-15W

EQUIPMENT

TENTS

CONVOY

6 MISSILE TRAILERS

TENTS

14

ABOVE: U-2 images of an area of Cuba near San Cristobal, October 14, 1962, showing convoys with Russian missiles which sparked the Cuban Missile Crisis. (CIA)

ABOVE: The Hycon 73B camera of the type used to obtain images over Cuba during the days of tension in October 1962. (NASM)

was introduced in 1958, providing the CIA with one of the ground breaking technology developments of the time.

OVERFLIGHTS

When flight operations with the U-2 began, the CIA and the Air Force believed it could fly undetected over the Soviet Union but many thought it had a year at most before Russia developed anti-aircraft missiles to bring it down. Because of this, the CIA planned a large number of missions to get the most out of the project, considered interim at best, hence the priority to get strategic results. But the optimism of the CIA was short-lived after the Russians immediately detected the aircraft and made numerous diplomatic protests.

The first overflight was made in 1956 and continued until Gary Powers was shot down on May 1, 1960, and of the 24 missions conducted over the territory of the Soviet Union, six originated in Germany, three in the Far East and Alaska and 15 from Turkey and Pakistan. More than 1.285million ft (391,668m) of film was developed covering 1.3million square miles (3.3million square km), or 15% of the Soviet Union, information which produced 5,425 separate analytical reports, according to the CIA, detailing the false claims by Russia that it had military superiority over the United States.

During the 1950s, political opponents of the Eisenhower government claimed that Russia was out-producing America in long-range bombers capable of attacking the United States. This was followed by a claim that the Russians were racing ahead with nuclear-tipped, long-range strategic missiles. The secret spy missions provided the government with abundant evidence that this was not the case, although it was not possible to publicly contradict the politically motivated claims for fear of disclosing the full breadth and extent of how this information had been obtained. The only disclosure came in CIA testimony to Congress in May 1960 that "the Soviet ICBM program has not been and is not now a *crash* program" (emphasis in the original).

What was not disclosed was the great advantage the CIA programme had

for updating and correcting maps and geophysical information held at that time by the military from old maps dating back to World War Two, which had been obtained from the Germans as they re-mapped the country. But these were not perfect and with accurate targeting essential for contingency planning in the event of war with Russia, the U-2 pictures, and additional information obtained from other aircraft flying near to or across the border, the US military was able to more effectively plan operations that may have been required for a future conflict.

It is difficult to overestimate the value of the subsonic U-2 and its successor, the Mach 3+ A-12, with major technology advances which also produced unique imaging capabilities. In service for operational missions until retired in 1968, the A-12 could accommodate three optional camera systems. Referred to by the CIA as the 'Package', the Type I system was built by Perkin-Elmer and occupied the Q-bay in the fuselage camera housing which was capable of uncaged operation where the assemblies maintained orientation with relation to the ground irrespective of minor attitude excursions due to turbulence or small course corrections. The quartz glass material protecting the cameras had to be optically pure and was inverted for that purpose, a hatch at the top of the Q-bay for accessing the equipment on the ground and loading film or changing components.

Although the aircraft could operate at altitudes of up to 90,000ft (27,400m), the normalised runs were conducted at 80,000ft (24,400m) at which height a swath covered a width of 86miles (138km) with each of the two cameras in the assembly having a swath of 67deg from vertical, the forward one nodding to the left and the aft one to the right. The cycle time for stereo pairs was

ABOVE: The restricted space in a U-2 is displayed by award-winning photographer Christopher Michel as he flies at an altitude of 70,000ft (21,336m). (Christopher Michel)

ABOVE: The Mach 3 Lockheed A-12 Oxcart, this example of which was lost over the South China Sea on June 6, 1968. (USAF)

4.8sec and film capacity allowed for 900 pairs with integrated data notations. For some missions, several runs over the target were made with each pass lasting approximately four minutes. The entire system was shock-mounted in the Q-bay and usually carried in the caged position until needed.

Tests and operating trials, development runs, calibration flights and training missions were run out of Area 51and activation of the operational A-12 detachment in early 1967 took place at Kadena AFB, with processing of the exposed film conducted by Eastman-Kodak in New York. From the standard operating altitude, ground resolution was a remarkable 12in (30.5cm) in the vertical. Other systems were available when required, such as the Type II built by Eastman-Kodak and the Type III by the Hycon Corporation. Between 1962 and 1968, the 15 A-12s made 3,017 flights totalling 5,080.9 hours in the air. Nine survived to be on display as the world's most exotic, highest flying and fastest spy-plane ever built, succeeded by the Air Force's SR-71 Blackbird.

Information about the strategic situation in the Soviet Union was essential to measuring the strength and capabilities of Russia's industrial and military might. But it would not come through overflights, which were mainly useful for providing information on selected bases, airfields and ports. Concerns about the risks inherent with aerial overflights predated the development of the U-2 and more still of the A-12. When he became President in January 1953, Eisenhower expressed concern over inadequate intelligence regarding Russia and its capabilities and of the *ad hoc* way in which local military commanders were conducting their own penetration mission to gather intelligence about Russia and China.

At Eisenhower's urgings, at the end of 1953 the US Air Research and

Development Command (ARDC) proposed a satellite-based spy camera long before the prospect of a space programme had been accepted for future planning purposes. In fact, long before the general public seriously considered the use of orbital flight as a practical possibility. But the test and deployment of medium and long-range rockets was underway and both the Air Force and the Army recognised that command of the ultimate 'high ground' would determine the future domination of Earth. For more immediate applications, the possibility of a spy satellite seemed plausible.

If the challenges in flying a camera designed to provide high resolution photographs from 60,000ft (18,290m) with the subsonic U-2 were daunting enough, the prospect of returning useable photographs to Earth from a capsule in space travelling at more than 17,000mph (27,350kph) were almost beyond existing capabilities. By 1955, however, such a programme was funded and under development while a parallel, civilian

satellite programme had been approved as a precedent for flying over countries sensitive to aerial overflights.

SPYING FROM SPACE

Under the codename CORONA, the first spy satellites were launched in 1959, two years after Russia launched the Space Age with its Sputnik satellites and the United States had followed with a range of science probes of its own. Camera systems would evolve over time, initially using the codename Keyhole (KH) and with a suffix number to indicate the generation, starting with the KH-1. At first the CORONA satellites used a 24in (61cm) focal length camera with 70-mm acetate film producing a resolution of 170 lines/mm.

The camera assembly was carried on the front end of an Agena rocket stage which took over when launched by a Thor rocket to propel itself and the payload into orbit from where it was orientated for imaging runs along the satellite's ground track. The exposed film ran forward to a capsule

ABOVE: A modified A-12 re-designated M-21 carrying an unmanned Mach 3.3 D-21 photo-reconnaissance platform with a maximum altitude of 90,000ft (27,430m) and a range of 3,000miles (5,600km). (CIA)

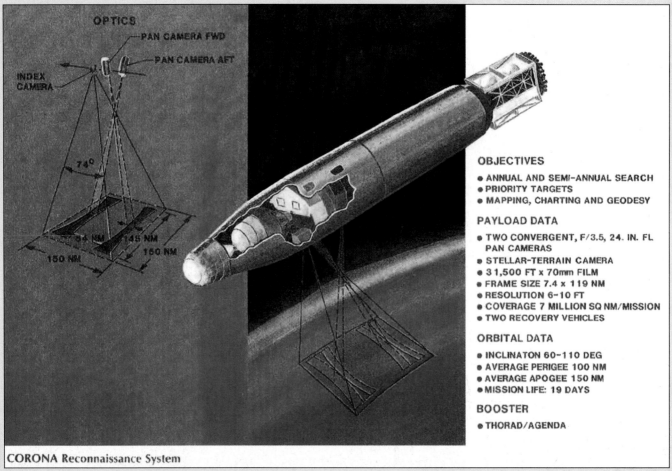

OPTICS

PAN CAMERA FWD

PAN CAMERA AFT

INDEX CAMERA

74°

84 NM   145 NM

150 NM   150 NM

OBJECTIVES

- ANNUAL AND SEMI-ANNUAL SEARCH
- PRIORITY TARGETS
- MAPPING, CHARTING AND GEODESY

PAYLOAD DATA

- TWO CONVERGENT, F/3.5, 24. IN. FL PAN CAMERAS
- STELLAR-TERRAIN CAMERA
- 31,500 FT x 70mm FILM
- FRAME SIZE 7.4 x 119 IN
- RESOLUTION 6-10 FT
- COVERAGE 7 MILLION SQ NM/MISSION
- TWO RECOVERY VEHICLES

ORBITAL DATA

- INCLINATON 60-110 DEG
- AVERAGE PERIGEE 100 NM
- AVERAGE APOGEE 150 NM
- MISSION LIFE: 19 DAYS

BOOSTER

- THORAD/AGENDA

CORONA Reconnaissance System

ABOVE: The Corona spy satellite systems were based on the Agena upper stage to which was attached a camera system and recovery capsule for returning the exposed film to Earth. (CIA)

which, when full, was separated and a small retro-rocket fired to bring it out of orbit where it could be recovered by an adapted recovery aircraft with a snagging line to snare it in mid-flight. The film canister would be delivered for processing, analysis and interpretation. The full sequence required precise timing for the launch, highly accurate positioning in orbit and clear skies to get useful photographs.

Over time the satellites got bigger, a second recovery capsule increasing the number of photographs taken, and the cameras got better, delivering higher resolution. Initially, Fairchild and Itek produced separate generations of camera equipment. Between 1963 and 1967, the high-resolution KH-7 GAMBIT series of spy satellites produced high quality photographs in which more than two-thirds of the pictures returned showed objects on the ground no larger than 36in (91cm), providing the CIA with outstanding results and a clear indication of Russia's military and industrial capability.

Between 1966 and 1984, the KH-8 GAMBIT-3 system carried four cameras and provided images with a ground resolution down to the theoretical maximum, about 2-4in (5-10cm) for specific targeting of particular areas identified as of special interest. The results drove the CIA to redefine the capabilities of the next generation but with the greatly expanded capacity to carry four recoverable film capsules in its KH-9 HEXAGON satellite, which was a much bigger, completely self-contained structure launched by a more powerful rocket. HEXAGON was the ultimate film-return spacecraft and flew 19 successful missions out of 20 attempts between 1971 and 1984.

Concurrent with HEXAGON, the disadvantage of delayed film-return capsules had prompted development of the next-generation concept which could directly transmit to the ground images obtained in space without waiting for exposed film. This was the KH-11 KENNAN/CRYSTAL family of spy satellites which emerged after

CORONA J INBOARD PROFILE

FILM PATH

CUT & WRAP

SUPPLY SPOOLS 180° SO-132

#1 RECOVERY SYSTEM

#2 RECOVERY SYSTEM

FAIRING EJECT SURFACE

1 MILLISECOND CLOCK

PERFORMANCE 125 NM
SO-132 125 L/MM 10°
COVERAGE 13.6 M NM²/FLT STEREO

J-1 TEMP. KEY-°F

FLT. HI/FLT LO. (M21 FLT.)
PRED. HI./PRED. LO.

FLT. MEAN (M21 FLT.)
PRED. MEAN

CORONA M CAMERA SUBSYSTEM
24" f/3.5 70° SCAN ANGLE
180 NM SWATH

12' - 1"

ABOVE: The ultimate development of the Corona-series carried two film recovery capsules, improved cameras and extended operational life together with orbital manoeuvring. (CIA)

ABOVE: On September 19, 1968 a KH-8 GAMBIT satellite took this photograph of Russia's N-1 rocket developed to put humans on the Moon ahead of America's Apollo programme. (USAF)

several decades of development and test with this type of delivery. Along the way, other types of image had been obtained from dedicated satellites, including infra-red cameras on some and radar images on others which are capable of providing pictures under local night conditions and through cloud and fog, 24/7 throughout the year.

But KH-11 was an altogether different spacecraft and used the same basic configuration as NASA adopted for the Hubble Space Telescope., except for the optics. First launched in 1976, KH-11 did not usually operate alone but in conjunction with the KH-9 and with a new generation of synthetic aperture radar satellites in a constellation of intelligence-gathering activity, providing immediate and comprehensive data through digital services. The ability to get direct and immediate imaging and other information from a range of different orbits attracted greater use of these systems, adding immeasurable quantities of data to a global compilation of reference information from earlier generations of spy satellite.

The use of satellites to obtain information about military and industrial capabilities of foreign countries provided a major expansion in knowledge and during the Cold War it produced highly detailed inventories of Soviet weapons and their capabilities. Backed up by listening posts close to the Soviet border, particularly in Turkey and Iran, the images and signals obtained from space allowed the secret Soviet war machine to be unravelled and defined. This led to arms reduction talks beginning under President Nixon in the early 1970s and continued under President Reagan during the 1980s. Since the collapse of Soviet communism, attention has refocused on today's perceived threats due to territorial ambitions asserted by China, by a belligerent North Korea and

by further claims from certain countries in the Middle East.

Russia was equally energetic in the early development of spy satellites and has developed a capability for photographic, digital and radar-imaging as has the United States and other major state players. Today, the use of satellite-derived intelligence information is key to accurately determining military operations, deployment, activation of new defence equipment and the industrial capacity of foreign countries and it is also a vital prerequisite for successful operations on the battlefield. So much so that anti-satellite capabilities have been developed by the United States, Russia and China is demonstrating that it has that potential too.

The reliance placed on satellite-based intelligence complements information gathered by spies and agents working on the ground in foreign countries and by land, sea and air-based sensors removing the fog of opacity that had for so long obscured the intentions of armies and governments. On so many occasions throughout history, misunderstanding and disinformation caused incorrect interpretation and dangerous assumptions that have unnecessarily caused a slide to war. In an age of nuclear weapons, miscalculation can result in escalation beyond any prospect of restraint and there can never be too much information to prevent that happening.

For these and other reasons, technology has drawn back the veil of mystery and

ABOVE: Titan II ICBM in its silo. Spy satellites enabled America and Russia to agree on arms limitation agreements backed up by mutual verification of each other's missile and bomber forces. (Mike McBey)

uncertainty surrounding the intentions of foreign powers which is why so many of the resources applied to national intelligence are spent on this direction. That was recognised as a vital capability, which is why President Eisenhower formed the National Reconnaissance Office (NRO) on August 25, 1960, integrating spy satellite programmes from the CIA, the Air Force and the Navy, an office so secret that it remained outside public recognition until it was inadvertently revealed in October 1973. It remains to this day one of the most classified of all US government intelligence agencies, headquartered at Chantilly, Virginia, and carrying the motto *Upra Et Ultra* – Above and Beyond, to see and hear everything.

ABOVE: A KH-9 HEXAGON spy satellite with four film-recovery pods. (CIA)

FUTURE-SPYWORLD

We live in a world in which information is more important than ever and through the use of computers, associated software systems and analytical tools, details of both a personal and a national nature are around us everywhere. Technology has utterly transformed the capabilities of government espionage agencies and all forms of human, imaging, signals, and electronic data-gathering are integrated and synthesised to build virtual 'pictures' of life at home and abroad, In an age where social media is a prolific self-declared index to an individual's life and behaviour patterns, the sheer blizzard of personal information is unprecedented, and the intelligence agencies use that to effect.

Today, satellites spy on other countries and keep watch on domestic threats from terrorists and subversive groups in society working to endanger the lives of ordinary people or bring down governments. They do this by collecting, filtering, and collating messages and signals of interest and on occasion most countries exert the legal right to electronically 'listen in' when certain key words and phrases are indicative of potentially dangerous activity, sometimes by their own citizens. So great is the volume of data that the challenge today is not so much to get hold of information, but rather to discriminate the useful from the useless and to focus on the former.

Human intelligence-gathering is as important as ever. Yet, as we have seen with the false messages sent back to Moscow by FSB agents fawning to their President with information they thought he wanted to hear

ABOVE: With the motto 'collaboration with strength and faith', the seal of the US Intelligence Community embodies a unified integration of civil and military agencies. (USIC)

about Ukraine's potential acquiescence to a Russian invasion, manipulated information can be dangerous. Which is why democratic societies separate the overall control of how spy agencies are run from the party prejudices of a particular government, and why levels of accountability and reckoning are cornerstones of a free society.

Espionage can be a double-edged sword and dictators are never sure that what they are hearing is a true representation of the facts. Bold indeed is the senior agency official who tells distasteful truths to a one-party government leader; Stalin never heard the whole story and Putin is often fed lies and misinformation, adding to a self-contrived delusion fuelling an aggressive hubris. In this way, nations can be carried to war as much by the type of information

they receive as by the nature of the reports put together by analysts. Which is why complex computer algorithms are at the core of data-gathering and filtering. In the United States, the NSA processes signals, while GCHQ does that in the UK. Each country has its own signals intelligence agency, and these are key to espionage operations in the 21st century.

Nobody goes into the intelligence business to make money, but there are many career opportunities for employment in these services of the UK, either with MI6, MI5, or GCHQ, each specifically focused as described in various places throughout this publication. MI6 provides positions on a wide-ranging scale and looks for strong interpersonal skills, languages, and some interest in technology. MI5 actively recruits through universities and provides positions in policy, project analysis, and legal work, in intelligence-gathering and data analysis, in technology development and in business-style management and administration. For technophiles, GCHQ provides positions in mathematics and cryptology, with specialised jobs covering cyber operations, analytical work, language interpretation and analysis and computer networking.

In the United States there are 18 separate and distinctly individual organisations collectively referred to as the intelligence community, several of which have been described in this book. Each has a unique mission; some are civilian in nature while others are defined by their recruitment through the ranks of military personnel. All agencies recruit at a wide range of levels and have graduate programmes with

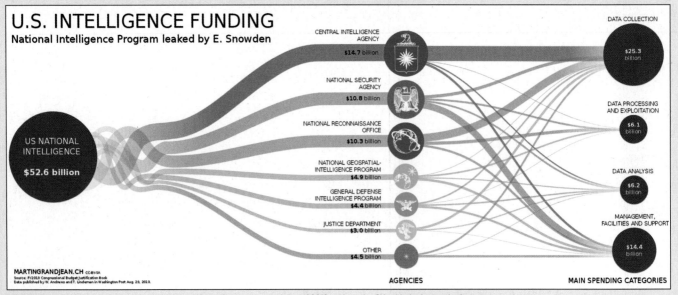

ABOVE: A snapshot of relative spending within the US intelligence community as of 2013 to show the CIA with the largest budget. (Martin Grandjean)

ABOVE: The insignia of China's spy agency, the Ministry of State Security. (China News Agency)

various universities while specific skillsets can sometimes attract attention from other agencies covering appropriate job opportunities. The core mission requirement for all agencies is universal throughout the free world democracies, that of wanting to make a difference and contribute to the security of the country of their citizenship.

Today, information exchange between allied countries forms an important part of ensuring a less entrenched view of international events and the Five Eyes group of the US, UK, Canada, Australia, and New Zealand is one example, common information with varied culturally diverse interpretations ensuring objectivity. As noted previously, Russia and China have signed a similar arrangement between their national intelligence agencies and there are known to be informal discussions at that level with North Korea and Iran, while Syria remains on the periphery with some intelligence provided by its own agency.

CHALLENGES

In the last decade, the world has been divided into polarised camps of allies and competing factions, with uncertain relations and high levels of suspicion between them. Fearing that the West and its military might pose a threat to its sovereignty and seeking

to reclaim lands it once occupied long ago, Russia has begun a 'special military operation' against Ukraine. The undeclared peace between North and South Korea has invoked a level of suspicion in each about the intentions of the other, causing North Korea to develop a nuclear capability with missiles and aircraft to match. Uncertainty too about future intentions of factional groups in the Middle East has brought its own tensions between people who share a common heritage and who, at one time, lived in harmony. There has never been a time when countries around the world have placed greater emphasis on information and the gathering of intelligence, even during the Cold War.

Some of the contested spaces are brought into tension for both territorial and economic reasons, tinged with a repurposing of national identity and the desire for greater influence in contested places. Having embraced communism and developed its own hybrid form of capitalism, China is seen by many as the global powerhouse of the future, while others fear it as power-hungry behemoth intent on dominating the great powers of the present with its own influence around the world. All these issues challenge the current state and capabilities of global espionage and intelligence-gathering and bring new urgency and the imperative for accurate and balanced analysis. But there are concerns that the national intelligence apparatus can be turned inward by a country aware that it can be overthrown from within, as China was immediately after World War Two.

China has achieved a technological superiority in operating networks that blanket the entire country and has chosen a labour-intensive route to sifting and filtering information about its citizens and those in foreign countries with whom it does business. The core of this is the list of several million informers encouraged by the state to report activities and people critical of the communist, one-party regime. This has worked well for monitoring internal activity, but it is not exportable and limits

the amount of intelligence obtained from foreign countries. And it is very expensive. In 2022, China spent an estimated $202bn on domestic security, which is equivalent to its entire defence budget. And the cost is growing. Its Sharp Eyes facial recognition system cost $40bn for equipment and installation alone.

Increasingly, China relies on a societal and institutional expectation that every citizen has a responsibility to report transgressions against the state or suspicious activity deemed to be challenging the authority of the government. During the Cold War, East Germany's infamous Stasi had one police officer for every 165 citizens; China has one security official for every 14,000 Chinese. Western intelligence agencies believe that there are up to 15million 'citizen-informants' in addition to the paid police and security forces. ID cards are at the core of this localised control, where they must be registered in shops and Internet cafes before transactions can be completed.

As China's global influence has grown inexorably in the last several decades, and with its economy heavily reliant on trade and manufacturing, its overseas espionage activity has increased at pace. The Ministry of State Security is primarily responsible for conducting spying activity, cyber espionage, and collecting information on foreign countries and companies, while other organisations focus more directly on military and counter-intelligence operations. China is engaged on a major expansion of its military potential and seeks technological development to produce a more extensive defence infrastructure from nuclear missiles to land, sea, and air warfare.

Interestingly, rather than using illegals as practised by Russia to obtain information about restricted foreign programmes, China appears to prefer recruitment of academics and specialists in other countries and through contacts at international symposia and seminars. This has caused some concern among Western intelligence agencies as China appears to have conducted unprecedented levels of cyberattacks on

BELOW: China's Ministry of State Security has its headquarters at 100 Xiyuan, Haidian District with officers across the country and its staff operating out of every Chinese Embassy across the world. (Author's collection)

ABOVE: The future headquarters of America's Cybersecurity and Infrastructure Security Agency on the St Elizabeth's Campus, Washington, DC. It is a component of Homeland Security, which monitors cyber-attacks by individuals and state-sponsored agencies. (DHS)

companies, governments, and organisations in pursuit of national, economic, or commercial advantage. These are the fundamental objectives of every intelligence organisation, but the expansion of China's alleged activity in this area has raised unprecedented concerns throughout the non-communist world.

FUTURE-TECH

The basis of most intelligence-gathering objectives is knowledge gained through information and increasingly that result is achieved through electronic and computer processing. Data banks are required to store very large quantities of information and high levels of processing power are needed to make use of that in an effective way. That usually requires the use of complex

computational algorithms to move the data around, compare it with other electronic sources and produce a result. It is an increasingly challenging task which takes the human elements to a different level. Instead of sending spies into foreign countries as the only means of gaining information about another state, computer scientists and machine-learning technologists have taken over some of that work.

But computers and the processing power they provide are limited and the number of computations is finite. The most powerful computer in the world is the Frontier system located at the Oak Ridge National Laboratory, Tennessee, which requires 22.7MW of electrical power to operate. Computing power is rated in petaflops, each rated at one-thousand trillion (one

quadrillion) floating point operations per second. With 8.7m cores, Frontier has been rated at 1,194 petaflops per second, an almost unimaginable number.

Frontier, and other computers of less capability, are used for deciphering codes of physical reactions in matter and core atomic activity, extrapolating to unseen consequences in the natural world but sought, nevertheless, by physicists and others. They are not used by intelligence agencies, although in those organisations even Frontier would be inadequate for decoding the most complex, computer-driven algorithms for encryption or decryption. There are possibilities that exist beyond even Frontier and some agencies are storing data at great expense in terms of storage capacity and power requirements, against the day that much more advanced quantum computers become available for use by spy agencies.

Whereas conventional computers use the binary 'bit' as a base unit of information, which has to exist in one state or another, quantum computers use the qubit, which allows that unit to be in a superposition of multiple states simultaneously. The potential for building quantum computers is enormous, based on the power increasing exponentially with the number of qubits it contains. Google claims that its quantum computer can perform in six seconds a calculation that would take 47 years with the most powerful conventional computer. Most applications today focus on research in the pharmaceutical industry and in solving complex scientific problems.

But in the very near future, information wrestling, where opposing problem-solving equations battle each other, will produce a winner before the contest begins. It can do

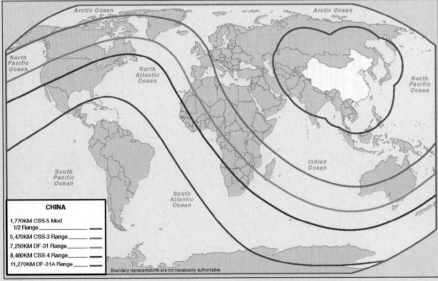

ABOVE: China has developed a wide range of ballistic missiles with the largest having sufficient performance to reach any potential adversaries. (CIA)

that because when the issues are presented, such as interpreting the complex actions of several billion separate information packets, the solution is found through means which would require more conventional computing hours than there are within a human lifespan. When those packets are individual data-points harvested through intelligence operations, solutions are critical to decisions based on that information. It is known as 'zero-tolerance error'.

Future-tech is moving data-collection to new heights too. Satellites gathering signals, be they radio messages transmitted between microwave cell-towers, human conversations snatched from the air, or complex coded transmissions, are getting better and smarter. Imaging satellites in the visible and radar portions of the spectrum are prolific for commercial and scientific purposes and the defence and intelligence agencies are increasingly using these sources for information which previously would have required dedicated satellites procured by governments at great cost. Most investment is now going into signals intelligence where both satellites and ground receptors harvest the vast blizzard of messages and texts proliferating the air waves.

New to the intelligence community are microbots, defined as being smaller than 1mm in size and capable of operating autonomously or in swarms, potentially in a coordinated way to provide information from inaccessible or dangerous places and across areas where humans cannot get. With receptors and processing power sufficient to send harvested signals and

BELOW: In the process of being installed at the Rensselaer Polytechnic Institute in Troy, New York, IBM has provided the first quantum computer on a university campus. (IBM)

images, microbots are of particular use on the battlefield, but they have many other uses for spy agencies too.

BACK TO BASICS

For all the abundance of high-tech equipment and vastly superior computer processing systems than anything available during the Cold War, the human element is still key to successful intelligence gathering, to sharing vital information with allies, even to assuring success against aggressive belligerents. Evidence of that comes from the combined operation between the CIA and MI6 in providing detailed intelligence to Ukraine's SBU spy agency from February 2014 when

the future of the country was uncertain and pro-Russia elements tried to turn it from looking to the West for its future.

It was the depth of information that the SBU provided to British and American agencies that began the relationship 10 years ago and which has enabled stiff resistance from Ukrainian armed forces in the wake of the Russian attack on February 24, 2022. After the pro-Russian leadership under Viktor Yanukovych left Kyiv for Moscow in 2014, the new head of the SBU, Valentyn Nalyvaichenko, occupied vacated offices and reached out for cooperation and help. At first the Americans were reluctant to engage with him due to concerns from President Obama

BELOW: China operates an ambitious space programme which it has developed internally, claiming that it will have its astronauts on the Moon by 2030. (CNS)

BELOW: Electronic signals Intelligence gathering is a vital part of understanding the intentions of a potential adversary, as conducted by this Oste-class ship of the German navy. (KleeBuchemer/Wikipedia)

that it might provoke Russia into an attack. But when Ukrainian military intelligence agency provided solid information from inside Russia, the mood changed, and the relationship was entrenched.

After two years of war with Russia, that cooperation is as strong as ever and even more effective. From 12 underground bunkers not far from the border, with support from the CIA and MI6, Ukrainian personnel provide information to the SBU which includes details of voice communications between Russian soldiers and their command centres, provides

information about the spacing of orbital ground-tracks for military spy satellites and details of troop movements. It is a two-way exchange, Ukrainian agents, having infiltrated deep into Russian territory from before the invasion, providing detailed information that now informs airborne strikes on military and industrial targets.

Based on human assets using technology to aid the Ukrainians, it is a very real and present manifestation of when intelligence and covert operations go to the assistance of a beleaguered nation seeking its own future unfettered by historical narrative

and the machinations of a neighbour intent on its subjugation, perhaps even its ultimate elimination as an independent country. This degree of cooperation using a wide range of assets has been copied in several countries and grows still as hostile intent increases and the demands on the intelligence services grow ever greater. National security and the safety of civilian life is the objective of every democratic society, even to the extent of informing the appropriate and proportionate use of military power to offset the numerical and strategic superiority of an assailant.

ABOVE: The listening ears of the Dutch Nationale SIGINT Organisatie (NSO) outside the village of Burum, epitomise the shift from human to electronic intelligence. (Wutsje/Eikimedia Commons)